DUAL RESTRUCTURING

Dual Restructuring

A Two-Way Route to Survival and Competitive Advantage

by
Dr Fritz Kröger
and
Steffen Hasselwander
Dr Carsten B. Henkel
Richard Hesch
Erna-Maria Trixl
Dr Odo Turowski

Dr Marianne Denk-Helmold (editorial support)

with contributions from
Dr Diethard Bühler
Dr Horst Größer
Stefan Krenz
Dietrich Neumann
Dr Heinrich Seidlmeier
Dr Michael Träm
Otfried Vogt

MACMILLAN
Business

Published by arrangement with Schäffer-Poeschel Verlag GmbH

First published in Germany 1994 as *Duale Restrukturierung*

English translation first published 1996 by
MACMILLAN PRESS LTD
Houndmills, Basingstoke, Hampshire RG21 6XS
and London
Companies and representatives
throughout the world

ISBN 0–333–67462–6

A catalogue record for this book is available
from the British Library.

10 9 8 7 6 5 4 3 2
05 04 03 02 01 00 99 98 97 96

Printed and bound in Great Britain by
Antony Rowe Ltd, Chippenham, Wiltshire

Published in the United States of America 1996 by
ST. MARTIN'S PRESS, INC.,
Scholarly and Reference Division
175 Fifth Avenue, New York, N.Y. 10010

ISBN 0–312–16509–9 (cloth)

Contents

List of Figures

Preface to the English Edition

Since its publication in November 1994 the book has been extensively discussed in Germany as well as within and beyond European borders. This has been reflected in press reviews in *WirtschaftsWoche*, *Manager Magazin*, the *Wall Street Journal* and *Business Week*.

Internal discussions within A.T. Kearney soon revealed that the dual restructuring concept could be applied – at least with similar macroeconomic consequences – to the division of value chains between North America and Mexico/South America as well as between Japan and China. The outcome in the medium term will be a changed pattern of value chains worldwide with growing wealth and increasing GDPs for all parties involved.

I would like to thank the authors and Dr Marianne Denk-Helmold for contextual and editorial review and Nancy Bishop of A.T. Kearney's corporate communications department for linguistic adjustments for English-speaking readers.

1 Dual Restructuring: A Two-Way Route to Survival and Competitive Advantage

Carsten B. Henkel, Richard Hesch and Fritz Kröger

It's an old story in the business news media: The competitive position of companies is in a constant state of peril. Whole industry sectors are in or on the brink of decline. Traditional markets have almost reached saturation. Foreign competitors put pressure on companies in their home markets in Europe, Japan, and the United States.

Due to high tax structures and high labour costs in Western Europe, companies in these industrialized countries are increasingly confronted with productivity pressure. In the USA companies have experienced similar pressures for many years, since the arrival of high-quality, cost-efficient products from foreign competitors. Today the aerospace industry, for example, is facing increasing foreign competition along with declining government defence expenditure, traditionally a mainstay of the industry. In the USA labour costs are also very high, although US companies have a slight competitive advantage over German companies.

In the meantime, Japanese companies are threatened by Asia's 'little tigers'. Labour costs are increasing in Japan, and the work force is less willing to drive toward 100 per cent quality performance. The Japanese standard of living is gradually moving toward that of the USA and Europe. Japanese products can no longer be offered at excessive prices in the home market to finance global expansion and force out competitors. Even Japan's once highly praised innovative capability is declining. Sony, for instance, the classic example of innovative power, generated huge operating losses in the fiscal year 1994.

In this situation, both traditional and new management fads and buzzwords fall short. Conventional parochialism has to be eliminated. It is not the time for incremental improvements. Significant breakthroughs have to be achieved, taking advantage of completely new strategic alternatives. The three major players – a group referred to as the Triad that includes the USA, Europe, and Japan – all have one thing in common: in recent years, huge economic regions with significant resources and huge market potential have developed on their borders. In Europe, the Iron Curtain to the East was lifted. The North American Free Trade Agreement (NAFTA) gave US companies access to stabilizing economic markets in Central and South America that are trying to follow the US model. The Japanese recall their own economic boom of the 1950s and 1960s when they now look at their neighbours South Korea and Taiwan. Mighty China may threaten or ultimately overpower Japan. The Japanese in this situation should offer support and alliances when China needs them.

Eastern Europe, South and Central America, and most parts of South-east Asia can be collectively described as emerging markets. Companies in these markets face huge problems. However, the most severe and significant problems are being encountered by companies in Eastern Europe.

Executives of these companies strive for fast access to western markets but are not yet capable of meeting market requirements. Their shaky current situation and uncertain future are reminiscent of the situation in Western Europe after the Second World War: The rapid growth of industry in Germany – later referred to as the economic miracle – was only possible through the significant support of the US government and US companies. There is no comparably strong influence in Eastern Europe today so companies have to seek completely new ways without knowing in which direction to look.

Chinese enterprises are in a situation similar to those in Eastern Europe, although political continuity is more likely because the communist system is still in place. The question of Deng's successor lingers, however. Chinese state-owned enterprises urgently need foreign technology, know-how, and capital to provide food and employment for the more than 1.2 billion Chinese inhabitants.

The current situation and constraints faced by companies in traditional industrial states as well as those in emerging markets strongly demand new remedies:

- Numerous western companies are not competitive. Cost problems offset even the smallest competitive advantage gained by flexibility and quality. Therefore, the performance of major western and northern companies often does not meet the expectations of the global customer.
- Many of the new competitors in the emerging markets are not competitive either. Their main problems are not high costs, but a low purchasing power in the home markets exacerbated by weak distribution channels, lack of expertise, capital, and technology, and not even a hint of customer orientation.

These complementary profiles suggest co-operation between companies of both economic regions. Interlocking the value chains can point the route towards a decisive competitive advantage for both parties (Figure 1.1).

- As part of a co-operative arrangement, a German machine tool manufacturer relocates value-adding activities to adjacent locations in Hungary, shedding low qualified jobs while creating new ones on higher levels. The advantages for the German company are significantly reduced labour costs and improved access to the developing East European markets.
- At the same time, the Hungarian companies gain employment and access to Western markets. In addition,

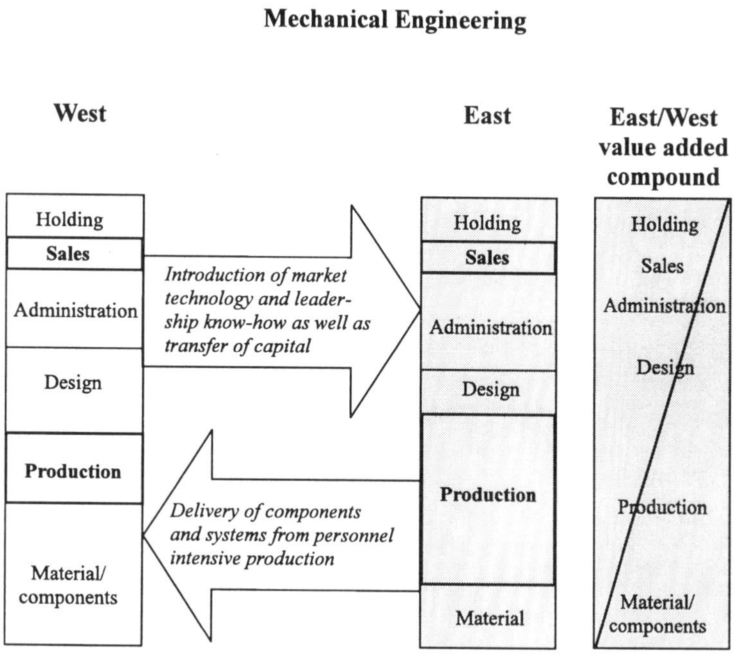

Figure 1.1 An example of dual restructuring (simplified)

they benefit from continuous knowledge and skill transfer, especially in the areas of marketing and sales. Thus, they outperform comparable companies who do not have western partners.

However, the necessary competitive advantages are only realized when both partners – Eastern with Western Europe, North with South America, Japan with China or other Asian countries – closely integrate their value-adding processes. This interlocking process demands significant changes in both participating companies, and this is called 'dual restructuring'. A comprehensive reconfiguration of the value chain will dramatically change the overall structure and boost the performance of each company in the chain. Both the underdeveloped company in the emerging market and the industrialized company that relocates and consolidates its activities must be restructured to the bones:

- the mature company reduces its vertical integration by relocating labour intensive, non-core manufacturing steps and focusing strongly on marketing and sales and product development;
- as part of the co-operation, companies in emerging markets streamline their manufacturing process in order to become quality suppliers. In the medium term, the target company will become the nucleus for economic growth in the overall emerging market through a targeted transfer of knowledge and expertise by the western or northern partner.

COMPETITIVE PRESSURE IS INCREASING IN THE INDUSTRIALIZED WORLD

Western European, US and Japanese companies operate in an environment of continuously mounting competitive pressure. Companies' success depends on outperforming the competition on the three critical dimensions of time, quality, and cost. This way they can supply the market efficiently and conquer new markets. A competitive strategy focused on just one of these three factors will fail. Thus, successful companies will improve their ability to differentiate themselves.

Costs

German companies employ a highly qualified work force – with generally strong educational backgrounds and a high level of productivity. According to the Institute of German Economy, the average German labour cost in 1994 of US$ 26.00 per hour was the highest worldwide. In the same period, labour cost in Hungary was US$ 3.20, a figure that is half that in South Korea (US$ 6.40) but four times the average cost of labour in Russia, Bulgaria, or Rumania (see Figure 1.2).

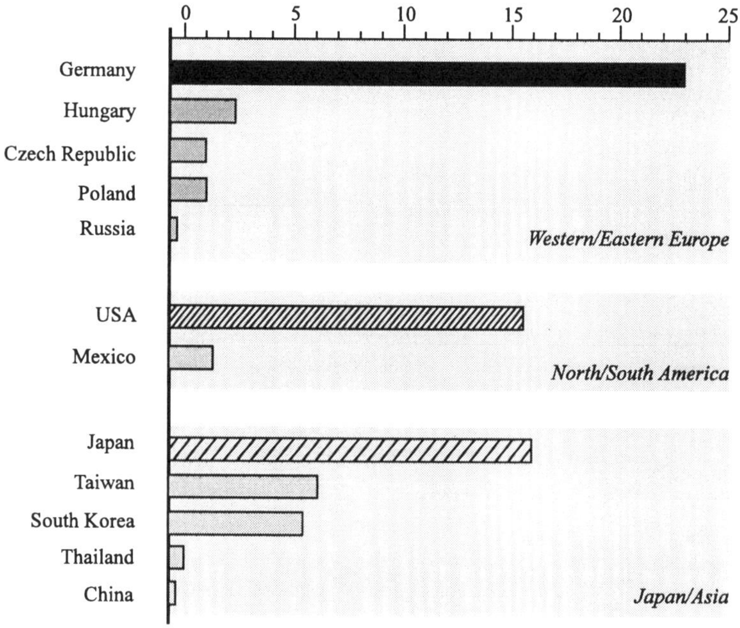

Figure 1.2 Labour cost, 1993 (US$ per hour)

To reach acceptable unit labour cost, even a leader in quality is forced to produce as cost efficiently as possible, because as a rule the quality advantage is quickly offset by competitors offering comparable quality at reduced prices.

Time

The rapid development of new products indicates that only the company that reduces time to market achieves competitive advantage. The advantage gained through the development of a high performance chip can only be sustained until a competitor develops a faster process and introduces a better chip. But being first to market does not secure survival. It allows only a short respite.

Despite the increasing need for flexibility, many companies have become complacent and bureaucratic as they have grown large and unwieldy. The movement toward lean structures is a long-term process and it results in people losing influence on processes. Until this optimization is implemented, the large, unwieldy company will not be able to meet the time standards (in turnaround and delivery) set by the competition and expected by the market. In other words, quick response to customer requirements by these bureaucratic conglomerates is unrealistic.

Meanwhile, smaller companies are more flexible, but flexibility and continuous innovation are difficult and expensive to maintain.

In addition to meeting customers' requirements on a strategic level, tactical reaction to market changes is necessary. The dominant market position achieved by the first competitor in a new market is difficult for other companies to overcome. This is illustrated by the market positions taken by the pioneers of the consumer goods industry in Eastern Europe – Philip Morris, Coca-Cola, and Nestlé will all enjoy long-term benefits from their initial flexibility and responsiveness.

Quality

'Made in Germany' once stood for a high level of performance that met and exceeded the standards of all competition. This image has changed. German automotive manufacturers spend time eliminating quality problems that occur during the manufacturing process while some Japanese competitors manufacture an almost perfect car in far less time. Comprehensive and proven quality concepts such as Total Quality Management (TQM) prevent most defects and thus help reduce costs; and, as these quality concepts are implemented, the 'old-fashioned' quality is seen as an expensive luxury.

Even companies in the USA and particularly in Japan that in the past managed quality issues well (measured in terms of customer satisfaction) are at a critical decision point: on the one hand quality is expensive to develop; on the other hand, many products can provide too much quality, in that the features are too complex for the general customer base.

Complexity is not a differentiating factor. Meeting the customers' quality requirements increasingly becomes a service issue, not a product issue. Technically brilliant products with impressive but superfluous performance characteristics are often produced in the interests of over-ambitious engineers, not as the result of customer demand.

Standard strategies do not work. Solutions are required that not only reduce costs, but that also dramatically redefine the company's cost position and enable major performance break-throughs. Customer-orientated business processes have to be redefined and redesigned. Existing re-engineering potential has to be realized. Reducing vertical integration through relocating low value activities to overseas countries with lower labour costs has been successful only to a limited degree for European textile companies.

Again, the situation in Germany provides an example of the new and exciting opportunity for dual restructuring. The opening to the East offers a huge potential with highly attractive cost structures and cheap labour just across the border. The common cultural heritage and the regional closeness to this economy provide a major advantage to German companies. They only have to make use of the existing potential to open new avenues for themselves as well as for the eastern economies.

EMERGING MARKETS REQUIRE STRONG PARTNERS AND INVESTORS

Western/Eastern Europe

The fall of the Iron Curtain was the most important event since the Second World War. The market-orientated western companies were suddenly presented with access to an economy of almost 427 million inhabitants covering Central Europe (the Czech Republic, Hungary, Poland, Slovenia, Slovakia); the former Soviet Union; and Romania, Bulgaria, and the former Yugoslavia. Despite the political, legal, and economic problems, the enormous potential of this region has yet to be fully exploited. But it is well recognized that economic growth and a relatively free market environment are prerequisites for political stabilization, which is also in the interest of Western Europe.

The eastern countries provide huge natural resources such as natural gas, oil, coal, and agricultural products, as well as a large and productive pool of human resources. More than 50 per cent of the population of the CIS – that is, approximately 200 million people – are well-qualified workers. Examples of the high performance of the former Soviet Union are its long-term leading position in the aircraft, defence, and aerospace industries. Valuable research and development (R&D) resources in the areas of metallurgy, physics, chemicals and electronics are available at one-fifth of the R&D costs in the West. The difference in labour costs is even more astounding.

However, the region is not monolithic in terms of economic strength or political stability: Hungary, the Czech Republic, Slovakia, Poland, Slovenia, and the Baltic States are regarded as more attractive for western companies than Romania and Bulgaria.

All eastern countries, however, confront major start-up problems, and the experiences and perspectives of western partners can greatly facilitate the development process in the East.

In addition, Eastern Europe and the Asian part of the former Soviet Union constitute exciting markets with pent-up demand for consumer and capital goods. The long-term development of sound markets can secure the survival of western companies and reduce the dependence on saturated western markets. Even when local buying power is insufficient, products and services from the West could be sold in exchange for products and services from the East on the basis of barter trade, provided that the quality level is adequate.

The investor and the eastern partner will both benefit from co-operation. Both consumer buying power and demand will increase. Pioneers from the West who have foresight have discovered that an initially precarious venture in the East can provide a long-term strong advantage.

Japan/China

Asia is the most dynamic growth region in the world. The former 'little tigers' are now well developed and are major competitors of Japan. China is still an unknown factor on the economic map of the world. German investors have only invested approximately DM 2 billion in this emerging market so far – a minuscule figure when one considers that the 1994 profit of Bayer, a leading German chemical company, was about the same amount.

China's 1.2 billion citizens still have to learn to be demanding consumers, but the key internal problem in China is a major gap in infrastructure, education and industrialization. The GNP per capita is only 1.5 per cent of Japan's (South Korea's is approximately 25 per cent, Taiwan's 34 per cent, Hong Kong's 50 per cent, and Singapore's 53 per cent). In addition, many rural areas in China lack paved roads, a telephone network, and above all even a basic industrial infrastructure. Conditions in the coastal regions are much better. Industrial output is mainly generated in the Beijing area and coastal regions like Liaoning and Hebei due to massive foreign investment.

China, with its huge potential market and its significant resources, presents a major challenge for all global players and for all international companies. Political instability causes a hazard for the years to come.

USA/Central and South America

The dominance of US investment in this region is demonstrated by the following figures: Of the US$ 66.6 million of

America's foreign investment in 1993, approximately 10 per cent was invested in Eastern Europe and Central Asia (representing an increase of 80 per cent over the previous year), 55 per cent in South and East Asia (up 75 per cent compared to 1992), and 24 per cent in Central and South America (an increase of 18 per cent compared to the previous year). Most (31 per cent) of the latter was invested in Mexico.

Many global companies operating in Mexico regard it as the platform for supplying all of Central and South America as well as the USA. For example, VW has a major plant in Puebla, Nissan has one in Cuernavaca, and so on. As far as population is concerned, Mexico with its 90 million population is slightly larger than Germany. Mexico's GNP per capita is 15 to 20 per cent of its NAFTA partners – the USA and Canada. Yet hourly wages in Mexican industry are about 10 to 15 per cent of those in the north. All Central and South American countries realize the advantages of joint trade associations like NAFTA. Mexico, Colombia, and Venezuela have formed an alliance – MERCOSUR – with neighbours farther south on the continent including Argentina, Brazil, Paraguay, and Uruguay. The main objectives of these associations are to eliminate trade barriers among the member states and to provide a joint political/economic approach to developing regional markets. Those who operate directly in one of the member states, for example, can usually enter other member markets without restriction.

Detailed analysis is required to answer these questions: Which activities are to be relocated to Eastern Europe, Latin America or Southeast Asia? How should one identify an appropriate partner? How should the co-operation process proceed? How should the restructuring and market entry process be controlled? Only with clear insights in these areas and with increased understanding of the requirements of the current and future markets can appropriate programmes be targeted and developed.

DUAL RESTRUCTURING IS A TRANSNATIONAL REMEDY

Through dual restructuring – or interlocking value chains – the value chain of a product is split between a primary company in the developed countries and an enterprise in emerging markets. The elements of the value chain are then recombined to achieve significant cost advantages and market access. The result is a new and all-encompassing pattern of labour division. The way to achieve this is the optimal restructuring of two complementary companies in both economic regions. All advantages gained by the support of the primary company trigger economic recovery and drive market development in the emerging market. Dual restructuring optimizes the performance through integrating the value-adding processes of both companies. This transfer of value added stages creates employment on both sides. It enhances the demand for highly skilled people in industry and services in the primary countries to serve substantially larger markets triggered by increasing buying power in emerging markets.

Dual restructuring roughly follows a three-step approach from the primary company's point of view.

(1) Analysing the relocation potential of value added activities

On the basis of cost leverage and strategic relevance within the value chain, all the value-adding activities of the western company have to be assessed in terms of their suitability for relocation to emerging markets.

(2) Identifying the location in the emerging markets

The primary company has to decide on appropriate countries or industries before the search for a target company is initiated. A wide range of factors has to be considered in selecting a target company, including the compatibility of cultures and manufacturing structures and the opportunity to contribute to the target company's competitive advantage.

The opportunities for entry into emerging markets have to be considered after a comprehensive product/market/competitor analysis. The result has significant impact on the location of the emerging markets, the selection of the country, and determination of the specific partner.

The form of the entrepreneurial venture in the framework of dual restructuring has to be defined for the selected activities. The range covers long-term delivery agreements with the target company at one end through to complete acquisition at the other. The decisive factor is the objective of the venture in the emerging markets. Is it the cost targets or penetration of a new market that is desired, or both?

(3) Implementing dual restructuring

Reallocating activities automatically suggests that the value chains of both companies are focused to create value for the customer. Both the activities in the industrialized region and those in the emerging market have to be tied together, leading to a new organization which implements new control and logistics processes. If both companies already produce high quality, reliable products, a sound supplier relationship is sufficient. A stronger contractual agreement is required if the target company has to go through a thorough restructuring.

Dual restructuring for these reasons provides a fascinating and challenging opportunity. Companies particularly well positioned to take advantage of this are those in mature industries such as

- steel
- machinery
- automotive industry
- wood processing and furniture
- textiles

In a dual restructuring relationship new value chains will be developed. Initially, the target company, as a supplier of low-tech products, components, and raw materials, will find its place in a worldwide division of labour while the primary company increasingly has to concentrate on high-tech products, design, engineering, and more complex services. In the medium term, the primary company will partially relocate its high-tech manufacturing and the associated knowledge base to cost-efficient locations in the emerging markets.

In the short term, these tasks require visionary new structures supported by detailed know-how on restructuring, comprehensive knowledge of the local conditions and the capability to implement the restructuring process.

The following chapters will demonstrate how and why dual restructuring solves problems for companies in both industrialized countries and emerging markets – through a process that energizes both companies.

The same approach is applied to dual restructuring between the USA and Central and South American companies as between companies in Japan or China and other Asian countries, but the trigger and strategic intentions will differ. West European companies have primarily focused on East European locations, mainly due to the cost reduction potential. In China, in some cases, the market potential may be the key initiating factor because of its huge size (even though there is likely also to be potential for significant cost savings).

Despite motivational and regional differences, however, the dual restructuring principle follows identical rules in all areas. Here the approach to dual restructuring will be detailed primarily through German–East European examples, because German companies are the primary ones currently practising dual restructuring with eastern partners.

Chapter 2 describes the situation for German and other Triad companies. Chapter 3 focuses on target regions and companies and provides detailed reasoning for dual restructuring. How to carry out dual restructuring is laid out in detail in Chapter 4, and three case studies are illustrated in Chapter 5.

2 Diminishing Strength, Increasing Weakness: Companies Need to Act

Steffen Hasselwander and
Erna-Maria Trixl

For a major company in an industrialized country, the term 'economic competitiveness' means different things at different times, and the meaning changes in relation to shifts in the country's economy.

- In periods of economic growth, the meaning of economic competitiveness is not debated. Corporate competitiveness is largely taken for granted because companies can maintain it by simply investing surplus resources in equipment and people.
- When there are major external pressures on economic growth, however, the term 'competitiveness' is broadly discussed, and it becomes inextricably linked to 'overhead cost reduction', which was much in evidence in the 1970s, during and after the international 'oil crisis', when reduction of indirect costs became an increasingly important management focus.
- Cost cutting was also clear in the industrialized countries' response to the market entry of Asian competitors in the 1980s. 'Reduce costs to *regain* competitiveness' became the watchword for any company unable to meet the new competitive challenges with its old organization and procedural structures.

Under any economic scenario, however, there is no commonly held meaning for the term 'competitiveness'. In practice, competitiveness is perceived to be the ability of a company to sell its products successfully. But success also involves delivering superior value to customers and providing 'shareholder value' in the satisfaction of shareholder needs. Concepts such as 'transforming the enterprise' through business process re-engineering and the creation of value chain networks are applied in support of objectives such as these.

GOOD, NOT EXCELLENT: BEST-IN-CLASS COMPANIES IN A PERIOD OF RECESSION

Attesting to the ambiguity associated with the concept of competitiveness, executives who are increasingly concerned about their companies' current and future competitiveness do not always have a clear understanding of how to become competitive or whether efforts to become competitive will be successful. They experience shrinking margins and declining revenues, and they want urgently to act to reverse these trends. But, in fact, these conditions need not be indicators of a lack of competitiveness.

An in-depth analysis of a company's constituent parts and all of its activities is required to gauge the potential for competitiveness. However, owing to scarce resources, excessive costs, or the lack of information on comparison companies, it may be difficult or impossible to perform such an in-depth analysis.

Ironically, companies often have detailed information from their sales force on direct competitors and their own position in the competitive arena; but, in many cases, this valuable information is not used to improve processes and thus to develop new competitive advantages. One factor contributing to this is that such information does not flow openly in many companies. Individuals in possession of valuable information on the competitive standing of their company and of competitors use the knowledge for personal power and not for the overall good of the company.

To build or improve the comparative data base to support internal analysis and improvement efforts, the company should benchmark its own activities by exchanging information with one or more companies that are related to it, though not directly competing. If the data sharing is done on an exclusive basis, all participants agree to non-disclosure; and, although the agreement can be breached, experience has shown that the benefit for all participants far outweighs the risk of disclosure of internal information.

One uncontested indicator of competitiveness is profitability above the cost of capital, and successfully urging for investment is another important aspect. Many companies tend to de-emphasize the latter. They confine their efforts to competing successfully in the market for their products and services while failing to optimize shareholder value. Yet higher profitability should make it easier for companies to free resources for the realization of future growth strategies.

Above average yield is both an indicator of current competitiveness and an excellent starting point for future competitiveness. But there are other determining factors on the verge of being introduced to the markets or a balanced SBU portfolio. However, while the relationship between yield and competitiveness may seem straightforward, determination and benchmarking of yield itself is a difficult process.

In evaluating competitiveness, the following results should be read as weak signals.

- *Shrinking return on sales* A declining return on sales in all industries over the past twenty-five years, as has been the case in Germany, provides an indication that market conditions have generally become more difficult. In 1968, for example, an average German company generated a profit of DM 1.00 from sales worth DM 32.00, providing a return on sales of 3.1 per cent. In 1990, the sales had to more than double – to DM 66.00 – in order to generate the same profit, dropping the return on sales to 1.5 per cent.
- *Reaching productivity limits* It is clear from a comparison of average annual growth in productivity that companies in many countries have hit the limits of their

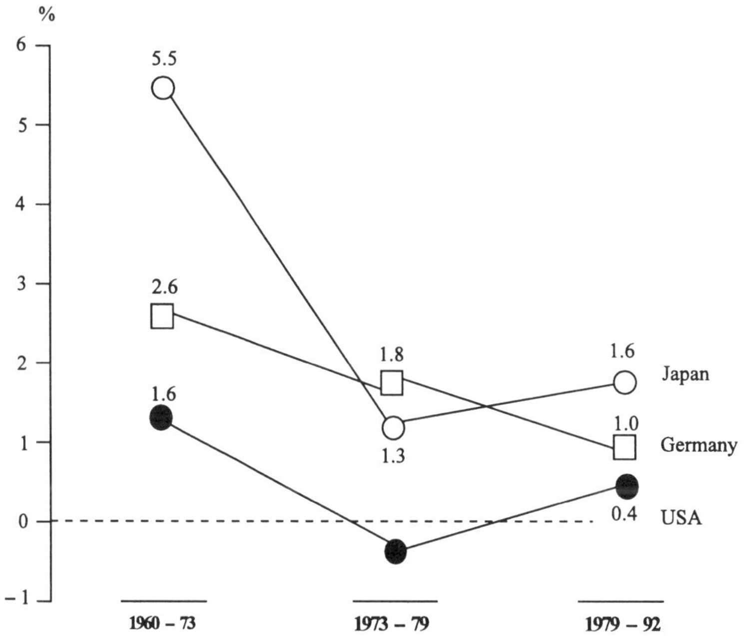

Figure 2.1 A comparison of average annual growth in productivity

productivity potential and certainly have not been able to re-attain the strong growth rates of the 1960s. The major exception here has been Japan, where productivity growth was both remarkable and alarming for competitors (see Figure 2.1).

- *Comparatively poor realization of export prices* Traditionally, the development of prices achieved on the world market has been a meaningful indicator of competitive position over time. Evaluation of performance against this measure shows that the current position of the USA and Europe is not encouraging after the 1980s economic expansion in the USA to the disadvantage of Europe (Figure 2.2).
- *Low output per employee* In Germany, during the period analysed, virtually all German industries have more than doubled the revenue per employee, some have

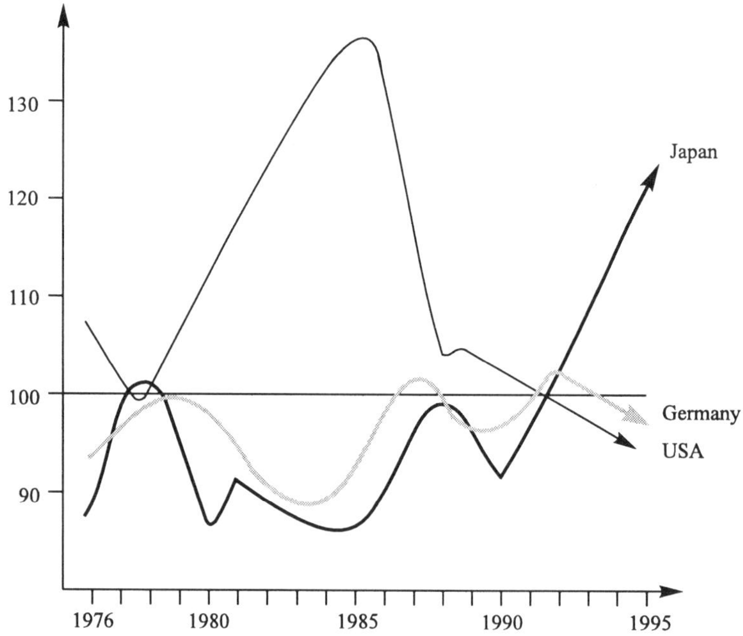

Figure 2.2 Development of export prices

almost tripled the ratio, and these are pointed to as indications of significant improvements in productivity. However, an analysis of the Fortune 500 companies in the USA conducted by A.T. Kearney in 1994 revealed that, on a comparative basis, revenue per employee in German companies is lower in all industries, across the board. This has significant implications for efficiency improvement in German companies (some of which may be found in streamlining administrative structures).

- *Decreasing gross sales in the international marketplace* Measured against the sales ranking of the 'Fortune 500' over the last thirteen years, the competitive position of German companies has deteriorated in international comparison; and it is in no way encouraging that US companies have dropped even further in the rankings from their previous highs.

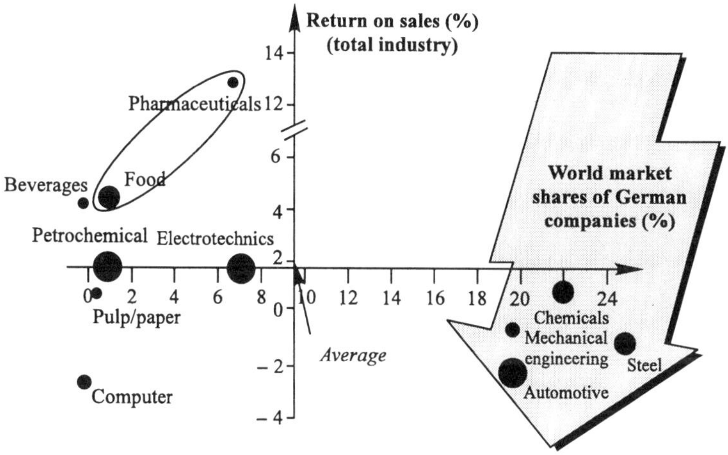

Figure 2.3 Weaknesses in strong industries

- *Weakness in strong industries, strength in weak industries* Again, Germany is a good example of this aspect of impaired competitiveness (see Figure 2.3). As compared to the Fortune 500, German companies have above average representation in the low-yielding industries. For example, in bulk chemicals, engineering, steel and automotive industries, Germany's major companies have a world market share of 20 per cent. These traditional industries generate 80 per cent of German industry sales revenue. Because these industries provide low yield, however, an increase in market share would not have a major economic impact. In the highly profitable pharmaceutical industry, however, and in a wide range of consumer goods industries, German companies now play a minor worldwide role.

So, there are some measures that can help signal a weakened competitive position in the international markets; and it is appropriate to assume that strengthening one's position along such dimensions as return on sales, productivity growth, export price realization, and output would have a correspondingly positive effect on competitiveness. But, however interesting and valuable these observations are, they do not provide a clear blueprint for action.

This is partly due to the fact that an extrapolation from historical data is often problematic in a dynamic environment – the path to past success may not lead to future success – and conditions are such today that a newcomer can move into a major international role through revolutionary innovation.

In addition, the data may suggest interpretations that are misleading. For example, strong current sales levels, and even return on sales, may in fact be poor indicators of future competitiveness. The foundation for a company's current success could be crumbling, and sales data would not reveal this. If the lead time between achievement of a product advantage and overall marketing success is long, many events and conditions can intervene to impair the company's future sales edge. If a company does not continue to market aggressively or if it fails to take into account the importance of customer loyalty, it may find its sales dropping from current levels as highly innovative competitors, who may be lower in the current rankings of sales and profitability, move in to capture market share with top products, cost-efficient delivery, and generally superior supply performance.

In Germany, there is a sense of complacency based on past success which has worked to damage the country's competitive economic standing and may compromise its ability to make future international strides. The majority of German companies still rely on a reputation established in the aftermath of the Second World War, but in fact this reputation began to erode as early as the 1950s and 1960s.

Excellent engineering performance in combination with the special atmosphere of 'awakening' after the Second World War were the driving factors of high productivity in Germany. Yet, competitive position cannot be retained on the grounds of custom solutions and traditional relationships alone. The German machine tool industry – a leading exporter for years – is a negative example. Japanese companies in this industry have succeeded in putting their

German competitors under pressure; and, in light of quantum leaps performed by the Japanese in such areas as cost and delivery, the Germans' former competitive position can hardly be regained through product and service quality alone.

Similar developments have occurred in other industries – Japanese and Korean companies have encroached on territories that German companies considered to be theirs. Through the development of international machine standards and particularly as the customer base is moving away from high-cost, speciality products (such as those offered by German companies, usually at excessive prices), the Japanese and South-east Asian competitors have succeeded in satisfying customer requirements at best cost through large economies of scale. There are only a few specialists left in the world who do not have to compete on the basis of price. The 'little tigers' and the Japanese are also competing in the custom arenas. But it is clear that buyers with their cost-efficient, price-sensitive, modular orientation strongly favour the manufacturing and supply companies based along the Pacific rim.

The Japanese have made similar headway in consumer goods. The initial objective of the Japanese automotive industry was to gain dominance in the compact car market through standardized high-volume products which could be sold at low prices. Initially, this caused disruption in the compact car segment of the German automotive industry, but people refused to believe at the time that buyers of luxury cars would ever fail to appreciate (and pay for) the technical excellence, the variety of accessories, and the high-quality design and reputation of a German product.

Since then, all players have realized that times have changed. Even before the Japanese manufacturers lost their cost leadership in the high volume automotive segment to the Korean competition, they began to concentrate on the luxury car market, while deliberately maintaining a favourable price/benefit ratio through cost-efficient modular assembly and minimizing the complexity of optional packaging. Because performance of these larger, more comfortable Japanese cars was on a par with German cars, the only problem remaining was to modify the perception that a Japanese car was by definition a compact car. The Japanese eliminated this problem largely by launching new brands and models with a special appeal of their own.

In summary, machine tools, automobiles, and a wide range of other products have been the subject of severe cost competition, and some German companies have turned losers. In addition, German companies have not reacted in a way that has improved their competitiveness – enhanced competitiveness will not come from delivering traditional products without cost reduction.

In other words, existing products at old prices cannot open new markets. The greater the number of companies competing in a market segment, the more difficult it is to increase new sales potential. Today, the international marketplace is characterized by competition among many suppliers, where even as recently as ten years ago just a few competitors dominated. Thus, the markets have become buyers' markets, and the demand of these buyers is satisfied by a highly flexible international supply network. Because the suppliers are offering goods and services that are comparable in many respects, cost competition is severe.

Despite the increasingly complex global market, there may still be a chance for a company to differentiate itself from the competition, but the 'time window' for pursuing such a differentiation strategy is closing, particularly in light of product life cycles that are becoming shorter and shorter. And, as suggested earlier, if strength through differentiation is preserved in weak industries, where the payback is low, the impact will not be significant. The only real opportunity today for long-term market success is for new 'star' products.

ONLY THE FASTER, HIGH-VALUE COMPETITORS WILL REMAIN SUCCESSFUL

For German automobile manufacturers and consumers, quality and high price have been inextricably linked for decades. It has taken a long time for consumers to be able to consider a Japanese medium-priced car as high quality, even though in actuality it might be comparable to a high-cost German product. But finally this trend is affecting the German consumer market and it has spread around the world.

In the USA, consumers have come to question the high-cost luxury segment on a large scale. Consumers refuse to pay an extra premium for additional accessories in the luxury segment in line with the increasing comfort provided in the medium-size segment. BMW has been able to forestall this development in the German market. The acquisition of an 80 per cent interest in the British Rover company in February 1994 was communicated to the market as 'a strategic decision to complete the product range with smaller and less expensive cars'. Mercedes–Benz, perhaps the world's most prestigious maker of luxury cars, has embarked on a fundamental re-alignment of its new product strategy. By the late 1990s, the company will have launched, among other models, a small family car, sized between a Volkswagen Golf and a Ford Fiesta and, most surprisingly, a micro compact car, a two-seater car for urban commuting that it is developing in a joint venture with SMH, the Swiss maker of Swatch watches.

Consumers' increasing concern about price–performance ratios and their demand for reasonably priced quality products is reflected in the sales figures of the leading UK retailer Sainsbury. The sales volume of its private label brand of cola produced by the Canadian producer Cott is higher than the sales volumes of Coca Cola and Pepsi together. The quality of this beverage is comparable and sold at half the price. The chief executive of a leading German clothing manufacturer summarizes the trend for the German market: 'Consumers do not look for cheap brands, but they want to buy the good brands more cheaply.' (See Figure 2.4.)

Lately this 'value for money' trend has spread to Japan. Torpid consumers, long numbed by the notoriously high cost of living, which is on average 40 per cent above the level of other industrialized countries, are discovering the

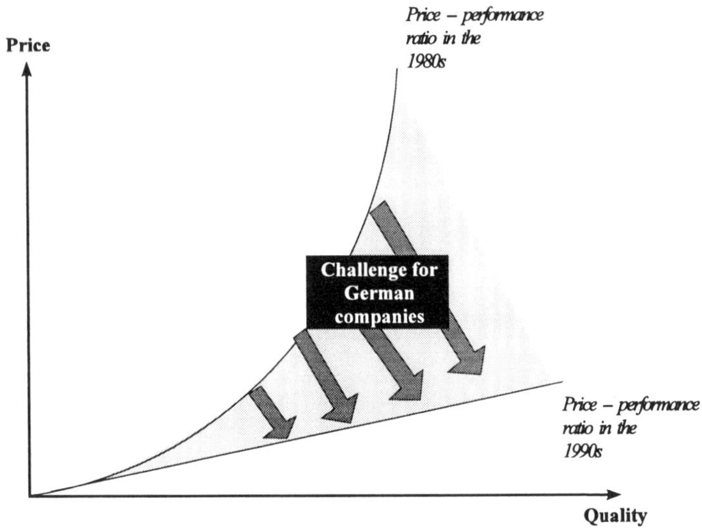

Figure 2.4 Increased market requirements as to the price-performance ratio

concept, so beloved in America, of value. They are revolting against paying high prices to subsidize Japan Inc.'s export machine. Much of the pressure for deregulation is indeed coming, for the first time, from Japanese consumers and their new-found price sensitivity. The recession is partly responsible for this growing cost-consciousness, as is the increasing worldliness of the Japanese. But what has really opened consumers' eyes is the increase in inexpensive, high-quality imported goods, made even cheaper by the strong yen, that are arriving in Japanese stores. The percentage of imported cars doubled between 1990 and 1994 from 5.1 per cent to 11.8 per cent. Suddenly, consumers have realized that they have been deceived for decades by protective regulations that compelled them to subsidize Japanese producers. They have become fond of discount stores and imported products.

Higher quality for less money is a sign of the times in standards for competitiveness. Suppliers who thrive on this principle raise consumers' expectations, thus creating a hurdle for their competitors. They prove that higher product quality is not automatically associated with better and thus more expensive materials, better and thus more expensive production facilities, better and thus more expensive quality control.

New quality process concepts present opportunities

Since the mid-1980s, companies worldwide have been striving for high quality products produced at low cost. The theoretical approach of quality concepts such as Total Quality Management (TQM) has become all but obsolete, but it is still practised in business every day. Total Quality Management does not only mean preventing failures instead of repairing defects. A flawless product does no more than meet basic customer requirements. It is certainly no longer sufficient to differentiate the supplier in the market. Therefore Total Quality Management focuses on customer-oriented quality and continuous improvement. To reduce total cost at the same time, the investment made to enhance product quality has to be more than offset by the savings incurred by eliminating failures and lowering defect rates. Reduced total costs result in higher margins, which in combination with an improved image enhance competitiveness. The latter in turn results in increased market share and margins. However, quality only works if it is integrated into an overall concept focused on customers and business processes:

- *Customer orientation* Companies that anticipate customer requirements and take customer satisfaction as the criterion for quality operate on a customer focus philosophy. These companies have the vision and capabilities to pursue customer-orientated innovation continuously – in addition to technologically induced breakthrough innovation – which is all the more important in times of ever-shortening product life cycles. If compared to breakthrough innovations which tend to be technical product innovations, continuous innovation has the advantage of requiring less R&D effort and incurring less cost. The shorter amortization periods are in line with constantly reducing product life cycles. Revolutionary innovation thrusts, however, take time and thus involve the risk that the high cost cannot be recouped in the marketplace.

- *Process orientation* For employees to feel responsible for the quality of the end product, they have to be familiar with customer requirements. In most companies customer requirements are known only by those employees who work directly with customers. By the same token, responsibility for value delivered to customers (that is, the company's product and services) is split among a multitude of individuals. For information, material and decision flows to run smoothly across the company, rigid functional work distribution has to be displaced by process-orientated co-operation in interfunctional teams. In leading companies, new products are developed in teams staffed with employees from the R&D, engineering, manufacturing, marketing and customer service departments in order to take into account customer requirements and other aspects, such as serviceability.

Even in a process-orientated environment based on cross-functional teams, there will still be interfaces between the teams and functional departments such as R&D and engineering – which are a necessity in any kind of division of labour. Most quality problems originate at these interfaces. These quality problems need to be minimized. We refer to quality problems in the broad sense of the term: that is, not delivering superior value to the customer, meaning flaws in the product or in the way it is delivered, or not delivering the kind of value the customer is willing to pay for. Minimizing quality problems requires clear process ownership and a common sense of purpose. The process owner has to have a broad enough perspective to look beyond functional and departmental boundaries and to be familiar with all the activities involved in the successful execution of a specific process. Also, he or she has to be aware of customer needs and their changes over time and across increasingly fragmented segments.

Process orientation results in high process quality which in turn assures high product quality. Many quality standards, such as the ISO standard, operate on this principle. Certification of overall process quality has come to displace product-related quality control which was performed formerly by the supplier and the customer. Despite the fact that ISO 9000 is widely known, the notion of product quality relying and depending on high process quality has not yet penetrated all minds.

- Although Japanese companies excel at process quality, receiving ISO 9000 registrations is not easy for quality-conscious Japanese companies. The biggest problem for Japanese compliance is documentation. Though many manufacturers have adopted Total Quality Management, they have not rigorously formalized it, and this forces them into much front-end preparation before ISO auditors arrive. Nevertheless, corporate Japan is scrambling to climb aboard the ISO bandwagon, trying to gain quality recognition in Asia.
- Applications for the Baldrige Award, America's prestigious prize for quality, have slumped. In 1994, only 71 firms vied for a Baldrige, a drop of one-third in three years. Optimists believe that waning interest in the Baldrige Award is evidence of American firms' new-found self-confidence in the quality of their products. Indeed, a recent study by Boston University, Tokyo's Waseda University and INSEAD concluded that American companies have caught up with and overtaken their Japanese competitors in terms of quality. Others contend that the Baldrige's decline is more a reflection of corporate America's increasing tussle with quality. Even the most ardent adherents of quality of the 1980s are finding that TQM does not readily blend with wave after wave of restructuring, downsizing and re-engineering. And the

challenge of developing products and bringing them to market ever more swiftly – especially in high-technology TQM companies – adds to the strain. Except for devoted TQM companies such as Motorola, most managers still believe that cutting jobs is a more effective means of cost cutting than TQM. And the snag is that downsizing undermines employee motivation, a cornerstone of TQM.

- Customer focus is an issue for only 50 per cent of all German companies with more than 1000 employees; only 12 per cent of these companies have defined customer focus as an outright objective. The majority of these companies do not regularly ask their customers about their quality perception by means of standardized questionnaires. On average 15 per cent of German companies perform analyses on customer satisfaction. Despite the fact that the engineering and electronics industries are leading in the introduction and implementation of TQM, only 20 per cent of the engineering and approximately one-third of the electronics companies perform customer analyses. Customer interviews are seldom performed and if they are, they tend to focus on regulars who generally provide positive feedback.

The operationalization of quality objectives and performance measures is not only the responsibility of management but can also be performed partially by the teams which are staffed with representatives of all functions relevant to the specific business process. Yet it is up to top management to ensure that all employees are trained in the principles of successful teamwork and quality improvement techniques.

Once these principles have been put into practice, company-wide communication improves. Information is not only exchanged among the functional departments. Management also hands over relevant information to the teams and in return receives important feedback. The structured approach of the regular team meetings seems to enhance employees' readiness to exchange information.

With cross-functional teamwork and improved horizontal and vertical information flows, employees gain a better understanding of the interdependencies within a company and can assume more responsibility. The latter is a requirement for improved customer orientation and satisfaction. Customers are impatient when sales representatives provide them with information on product price and availability only after having checked with a multitude of people – often engaging several hierarchical levels – or when the information changes later.

For TQM to become effective, it is necessary to adjust compensation accordingly. Management's appeals to their employees to increase customer satisfaction, tear down functional barriers and to focus on quality will be unheard as long as salaries and other elements of the compensation package are contingent upon short-term sales figures and balance sheet data. Customer satisfaction and sales figures will correlate in the long run; there may, however, be a gap in the short run.

On the face of it, few companies succeed in improving their quality without increasing cost. On second glance, this turns out to be a problem of poor cost allocation rather than of the high cost of quality: companies tend to ignore the immediate follow-up cost of poor quality such as scrap, extra work, customer claims and warranties.

- Even less light is being shed on the long-term consequences of poor quality: that is, declining sales and market share. Independent of company size, indirect costs such as losses in sales and market share caused by failures in quality are not taken into account in Germany.

Table 2.1

	Error rate (%)	*Quality*	*Cost*
Check on process capability	0.00006	+	+
Random test	2–5	–	+
Overall test	0–0.5	+	–

- In Germany companies still tend to confine their notion of 'quality' to technical product quality. As a result, these companies focus their effort on the product development process and production but neglect customer-orientated activities in service and sales departments. Yet achieving quality improvements has to be a company-wide endeavour integrating all areas 'upstream' and 'downstream' of production as well as administrative and support activities. Although the majority of companies are aware of the fact that service quality is becoming an increasingly important differentiator in the competitive arena, TQM techniques are utilized only by a minority.

- American companies have significantly improved product and service quality while becoming more innovative and cost efficient. Nucor Steel has reduced labour cost per ton of steel to US$ 60, while the industry average is US$ 130 per ton. Lincoln Electric is the cost leader worldwide for welding torches and electrical induction motors with productivity of 250 per cent above the industry average. Harley Davidson has regained its competitive position for heavy motor bikes, which was lost to the Japanese in the 1970s and 1980s, through quality improvement and a simultaneous 70 per cent reduction of rework. These productivity improvements have been achieved primarily through accelerating production processes and preventing failures. Toward the end of the 1980s, Motorola improved its product quality and controlled its cost through a lead time reduction – from order entry to delivery – of 30 to 3 days for radios. The development time for portable telephones was reduced from 3 years to 15 months and assembly time from 40 to 2 hours.
- The absolute quality leaders are, however, the Japanese – at least as far as defect rates are concerned. They come as close to 'zero defects' as one can probably get. Their excellent performance record is traceable to high process quality. As for the second quality component – that is, permanently keeping in touch with their customers and finding out what they value and what they are willing to pay for, the performance of the Japanese varies across

industries. While electronics companies are highly customer driven, suppliers to the automotive industry tend to have lost sight of the end customer because they are so tightly integrated with their direct customers.

What is surprising about the above success stories is the fact that TQM companies have not only become better (in terms of delivering products of higher quality) and less expensive but also faster. A decade ago lead time reduction seemed to be only realizable with enlarged production capacities and/or increased warehousing and delivery cycles.

After companies throughout the Triad have identified the necessity of short response and cycle times, world-class quality and competitive cost and have therefore embarked on TQM and re-engineering programmes, US companies are now moving from frontline business processes to management processes. Japanese companies have been very successful at unlocking the efficiency and effectiveness improvement potential on the shop floor; now they have to come to terms with their white collar overhead. 'Coping with the high yen has made us realize that we have many components and processes that we can eliminate to get rid of extra fat and become competitive again', says Minoru Nakamura, a Nissan director and head of the Asia and Oceania operations division. In German companies, business process re-engineering is still less widespread than TQM. In addition high labour cost will continue to be a problem there and throughout the Triad.

Relocation and outsourcing can be a solution

Why complain about high labour costs in Western Europe? Let us take Germany as an example. Germany has achieved a stage of development that makes it unprofitable for providers to perform certain activities. Providers would be manufacturing below the poverty line if compensation for these activities was in line with the generated value. However, if providers were paid the wages necessary to make a decent living, it would be impossible to recoup the resulting product costs in the marketplace.

This dilemma is revealed each year during wage negotiations between employers and employees. Employers argue that low productivity improvements justify only low wage increases and that declining demand requires the release of workers. Union representatives point to the threatening loss of buying power to demand wage increases that are generally higher than what employers are willing to pay. To break the stalemate, the main objectives of employers would have to be the realization of the existing savings potentials to achieve maximum efficiency, innovation and the development of new businesses. Representatives of the workers union would have to stop claiming their seemingly vested rights and tell their constituencies what it takes in terms of skills and capabilities to be paid in accordance with the standard of living.

- Despite permanent efficiency improvement, some manufacturers regard it as impossible to produce standard components in Germany at competitive costs. A top manager of a German machinery company said: ‘In Germany we did not succeed in achieving quantum leap improvements in cost’, and decides to relocate the manufacturing of standard moulding parts to Eastern Europe, where he saves 50 per cent of production cost. Several machinery companies have already tried to benefit from the low production cost in eastern Europe: for example, the Hamburg-based Jungheinrich AG intends to relocate its production of DC motors to Brünn in the Czech Republic.
- The United States has similar problems, although labour costs are more heterogeneous and flexible. In the wake of NAFTA, electronics, computer products and telecommunications equipment have been entering the United States from Mexico twice as fast as they have gone in the other direction. Much of this material is coming from *maquiladoras*, the duty-free assembly plants along the USA–Mexico border. Economist Jeff Faux of the anti-

NAFTA Economic Policy Institute argues that the tremendous US–Mexican wage gap explains the phenomenon. 'Those of us who opposed NAFTA pointed out there was a fairly sophisticated manufacturing base in Mexico that pays peanuts, and the numbers bear that out.' Currently some 2200 companies have *maquiladora* operations. Many of these are well-known multinational companies, including Sony, Johnson & Johnson, General Electric, Siemens and General Motors.

- The major problem for the Japanese is their increasingly strong currency, which has hurt their competitiveness in export markets. Some argue, though, that in the long run the yen's strength forces corporate Japan to become even more competitive. And indeed the Japanese have been very successful at boosting efficiency and lowering break-even points through severe cost cutting. The main cost-cutting technique has been to shift production capacity to South-east Asia and to increase purchases of components from abroad. Nearly one-third of all cars and machines made by Japanese-owned companies now come from outside Japan. Almost one-quarter of Japan's manufactured output is made abroad, and this is expected to double by the end of the decade.

While pessimists argue that this overseas exodus will deplete Japan's manufacturing base, Yasushi Mieno, former governor of the Bank of Japan, contends that it is an appropriate redistribution of labour between low-wage countries, for making price-sensitive commodities, and high-wage countries such as Japan, for making high value-added products. Despite the onerous costs of doing business in Japan, some industries, especially those that make high-tech products requiring a lot of skilled labour, will almost certainly stay home. Says Fumino Sato, president of Toshiba: 'Where speed, technology and constant improvement are necessary to a product, Japan is still the best place to operate.' Indeed, both Toshiba and its arch-rival NEC have recently announced or completed billion-dollar computer memory chip plants in Japan that each claims is the most advanced in the world. Comments by German experts express the same thing – the German manufacturing base is not at risk. Complex high-tech components tailored to individual customer requirements will still be produced in Germany – at competitive prices.

The profits of Japanese manufacturers of consumer electronics have not only been squeezed by the yen's sharp appreciation but also by sluggish demand and falling prices. Japan's consumer electronics market has suffered from fierce competition and from the growing availability of cheap products made in countries with low labour costs, primarily in South-east Asia. With manufacturing costs that are among the highest in the world, Japan can no longer rely upon 'people-dependent assembly' but must shift to a 'technology and know-how-intensive production system,' according to Mr Haruo Tsuji, president of consumer electronics group Sharp. One of the consequences will be that R&D costs are likely to rise even further. As hardware is becoming less and less important, Japanese companies have to become providers of software and information.

Because of its record of success over a long period of time, the German automobile industry has failed to gear up for future challenges. In 1993, production of automobiles fell by approximately 4 million, or 20 per cent compared to the output in 1992. The key problem for the German automobile industry is overcomplexity caused by the excessive amount of variants offered to the customer. While leading manufacturers have for years fitted the same components in various automobiles, the German OEMs are highly individualistic in their development and production. The Frankfurt-based brake manufacturer Teves supplies the German automobile industry with more than 1200 different types of main brake cylinders. Only recently have Mercedes and BMW initiated joint efforts to reduce production cost. German manufacturers have just begun to follow the Japanese example and reduce their supplier base.

German OEMs have realized that they can no longer produce a wide range of parts and components in Germany at competitive costs. As the automobile industry continues to reduce the degree of vertical integration, the cost pressure is moving to suppliers. Currently, about 50 per cent of production costs for an automobile are generated by purchased parts. In a few years this share will increase to about 75 per cent. The manufacturing cost of the automotive supply industry is still about 25 per cent higher compared to worldwide competitors. The suppliers, like the OEMS, have failed to improve their efficiency.

Component manufacturers' return on sales are shrinking because the increasing cost cannot be fully passed on to the automotive industry. An analysis by the Deutsche Industriebank reveals that return on sales have been declining since 1989, even for major suppliers: In 1991, they achieved 1.5 per cent before tax; in 1993 all of them generated losses. Japanese component manufacturers, by contrast, have continued to expand their lead in quality control, which allows them to sustain higher prices.

As the board member responsible for purchasing at the German carmaker Audi puts it: German OEMs expect their suppliers to offer 'foreign prices' and emphasize this with the threat to purchase increasingly abroad. In fact, the share of imported components more than doubled between 1985 and 1992. When Ignacio Lopez was the responsible board member at Opel, the share of imported components increased to 50 per cent, which is also his target at VW. 'Made in Germany', which had been the equivalent of quality for decades at Mercedes, has now been replaced by 'Made by Mercedes'. In the future, Daimler board member Gerhard Liener will increasingly source Mercedes parts in countries such as Hungary, Poland, China, the United States and Mexico.

In particular, medium-sized companies are increasingly searching for new locations and partners for new production lines in low cost countries such as Hungary and the Czech Republic. The automotive supplier ITT produces wheel brake cylinders in Hungary. The tyre maker Continental vulcanizes its tyres in the Czech Republic and Portugal. AEG, a subsidiary of Daimler Benz, is currently building a plant for vehicle electronics in Mexico. Mannesmann is in the process of reorganizing its worldwide sourcing base: in 1992 plants in the USA, Thailand and Malaysia began operation; plants in Indonesia and the Czech Republic followed in 1993.

Despite cost cutting and efficiency improvement the automotive industry in Japan still faces grave difficulties. The latest car plant to open in Japan was the Toyota plant in Kyushu. Most analysts think it will be the last greenfield car plant that the country will see. According to Steve Usher, a car analyst in Tokyo, one-quarter of the vehicles made by the Japanese car companies are being produced abroad. By the end of the decade, half of them will be.

Japanese components manufacturers are also feeling the pressure to move production overseas into low-cost countries. 'In order to survive as component suppliers, companies have to follow their big automotive clients on their move overseas,' says Koki Oku, a director of the foreign trade company Jetro. Mitsuhiro Seki, professor of economics at Tokyo's Meji University, fears the worst: the country that was so disinterested in the international division of labour now has to adjust to a niche strategy overnight. This would not be a problem if anyone here were at all familiar with what a niche strategy is.

For the US automobile industry, the dramatic changes promised by NAFTA have begun to occur. Ford is spending $60 million to revamp its Cuautitlán plant near Mexico City to produce smaller cars and light trucks for global sales. The numbers are startling: Ford's vehicle exports to Mexico are up from 1200 in 1993 to an estimated 30 000 this year. Its exports of Mexican-made vehicles to the USA have jumped, too – up 30 per cent in the first eight months of 1995.

High labour costs also cause problems for some consumer goods industries. Between the early 1970s and 1993, about 2600 of the 5300 German textile and apparel manufacturing plants were shut down and about 60 per cent of the 900 000 employees have been let go. The remaining 340 000 employees have no job guarantee.

Whereas the textile industry has tried to fight the threat from south Asian low-cost competitors by increasing automation and is now confronted with the problem of poor amortization of its high investments, the clothing industry is characterized by high labour intensity: production in low-cost countries turns out to be essential for survival. The leading European producer of women's fashion, the German Klaus Steilmann GmbH, has outsourced 80 per cent of its volume. Other companies in the industry achieve similar outsourcing volumes.

Outsourcing in the apparel industry is mainly focused in south Asia, although Eastern Europe is more favourable for Europeans, particularly for companies pursuing a quality strategy with high-value materials. Eastern Europe's proximity is an asset for those that require a short lead time in order to be able to respond to fashion trends immediately. Quick response systems that immediately transfer customer requirements to producers so that warehouses can be replenished are useless if the lead time for transportation by ship from the Far East to Europe is six weeks.

The German chemical industry also has high labour costs – two-thirds higher than the USA and one-quarter higher than Japan. Competition from Eastern European suppliers complicates the situation for German manufacturers. Their product portfolios are made up mostly of commodity chemicals and they have too few sophisticated products that would command a price premium and give them a competitive edge.

The supply of chemical goods from Western to Eastern Europe has declined by 50 per cent based on a volume of approximately DM 12.2 billion in 1989. However, the East European chemical industry has significantly increased its supply to the west, based on a volume of DM 6 billion in 1989, despite decreasing production volumes. Increases of up to 80 per cent were achieved in fertilizers and plastics. According to Jürgen Strube, chief executive of BASF, this import pressure from the East will continue as long as these unsophisticated products can be produced there more cost efficiently. Strube assumes that Western European chemical companies will focus their investments in Eastern Europe mainly in the area of downstream plants for high value-adding production steps. In the area of basic chemicals, however, there are few indications of investment of modern western technology into production plants in Eastern Europe. The formation of joint ventures with existing plants is more likely. There is the additional risk that companies in the processing industry, like customers of the chemical industry, will relocate production in East European countries, thus having a negative impact on the customer base of West European suppliers of chemicals. Japanese exporters, by contrast, have benefited from shifting up market into high value-added products. This leaves them relatively immune from undercutting by cheaper producers.

Corporations are moving manufacturing operations – as well as more sophisticated operations – offshore to save money. To cope with a strong yen, Japan's corporate giants have no choice but to accelerate the migration of their most labour-intensive manufacturing to Asian lands that have lower wages and cheaper land. This expected surge of money from Tokyo has not yet occurred, but it will come, even if pressure on the yen abates somewhat. The reason: Japan's work-force is ageing fast. To support the elderly, Japan's capital must flow to fast-growing countries that boast an oversupply of young, energetic workers. Recently China has been attracting Japanese investors. In 1993, investment increased 58 per cent compared to the previous year. Japanese manufacturers currently invest more money in China than any other country. This included joint ventures as well as the establishment of new companies.

For a wide range of industries internal efficiency improvement will not lead to sustained competitiveness:

(1) Companies located in all Triad powers strive for these efficiency gains, and eventually they will hit their maximum internal improvement potential.
(2) With consistently lower degrees of vertical integration, the potential for internal efficiency improvements is decreasing as well.

(3) Suppliers from neighbouring low-cost countries will emerge as competitors for low-tech products.

The future winners of the competitive game will be those who forge intelligent value chain/creation networks. For the players, the secret is knowing what to do themselves and what to leave up to others, selecting the right partners in the right locations and stretching their performance improvement endeavours beyond their companies' boundaries. Linking up with suppliers from neighbouring low-cost countries accomplishes three things:

(1) It pre-empts competition from low-cost suppliers in domestic markets.
(2) It creates a competitive edge over all domestic suppliers that do not take advantage of the opportunity.
(3) It gains a foothold in markets that will become increasingly interesting when consumer purchasing power improves.

In light of these opportunities, Triad companies should not be put off by the fact that linking up with companies in emerging markets may require them to provide some restructuring support to bring the cost advantages to fruition.

3 A Strategy of 'Go East' and 'Go South' Creates Win–Win Situations

Marianne Denk-Helmold and
Odo Turowski

The movement of Eastern Europe to a market economy and the opening of East European society and its economic system to the West have enabled companies from the West to integrate East European partners into their global economic plans. It is clear to many that effective investment in and co-operation with eastern partners is critical to the positive medium-term and long-term development of companies based in the West. Similar partnering opportunities exist elsewhere, across borders that had formerly been rigid and restrictive. For example:

- with NAFTA, and the easing of tariffs and custom restrictions, the USA can now co-operate more fully with Mexico;
- in Asia, the biggest change is that China is no longer monolithic and inaccessible but more than open to western capital and approaches to doing business.

So, Eastern Europe is just one example of an area ripe for international partnering, but it is a good example, for now countries in the Triad (USA, Europe, and Japan) can contribute to the development of emerging countries while expanding their own wealth. With the rise of the Iron Curtain, many western companies began to evaluate the ways in which they could most effectively operate in the eastern markets, where there is already a history of positive working relationships, social and cultural affinities, and an overwhelming cost advantage. So, in the period 1989–90, when the Iron Curtain rose, enthusiasm abounded in anticipation of tapping into the huge growth markets in the East, promising wealth for all parties.

After early experiences with this new investment arena, the naïve view quickly gave way to a more realistic perception of current conditions. Western companies, which initially regarded the former COMECON countries as being very similar, soon recognized that there were many important differences among the countries, with each requiring a somewhat different approach. So, precipitous actions taken by certain companies hoping to expand quickly into these markets quickly did not consider the uniqueness of each country and consequently they turned out to be failures. Procter & Gamble, for example, although currently very successful in Europe, failed in its initial East European activities due to inappropriate pricing of some products. Quick wins were not to be easily gained.

Western companies began operating more cautiously, as was shown by the fact that most of the direct investment went into former COMECON countries that were considered safer and more secure. Hungary, which had received western investment since 1976 as a result of its Investment Protection Act, became one of the most attractive countries for new investment.

The preference of western companies for locations that had a favourable cost structure and markets with strong growth potential turned out to be complementary to the requirements of their eastern counterparts. A comparatively well-situated East European company, hoping to survive over the long term, was looking to build a close working relationship with a western partner in order to modernize product lines, strengthen the capital base, and increase skills in such areas as marketing and sales. In this situation, the concept of 'interlocking of value chains' became especially useful in fostering an understanding of how a new division of labour could bring added value to Eastern Europe. It was also clear that related growth in employment and income would further strengthen the new global orientation. This frame of reference was forming in all the other emerging markets that were beginning to attract capital from relatively better-off Triad players in their geographic neighbourhood.

EMERGING MARKETS NEED TRIAD INVESTORS

All three Triad regions are situated in close proximity to less developed regions which, in principle, face a situation of which Europe is typical:

- The situation in Eastern Europe after such radical change is characterized by opposing political and economic forces. In many cases, the political direction is still not clear. There are those still favouring the state-controlled economy who do not know very much about the western way of life and hide their inability to take risks in the belief that communism is better. Then there are those who have a tendency to try the western economic system, and these are generally people who are acquainted with the pros and cons of the western life style, if not in real life at least from the media.

For pragmatic, well-informed, and open managers of eastern companies, it is important in the coming years that they actively try to understand the situation, so that they can have a better idea about which changes are realistic. And, to the extent that there may be an interest in restructuring, the eastern companies will not only need access to western capital and markets, they will also need new role models. For example, West European companies and managers could play the same role that American companies played after the Second World War – introducing new business concepts and principles.

Adoption of those western models that are currently dominant will be critical to success. Only if the western-orientated eastern managers succeed in increasing the flow of western capital and entrepreneurial expertise will the integration of Eastern Europe into the value chains of the

West European market be realized successfully. If such models are adopted, new economic and democratic structures can become a reality within a realistic period of time and eastern companies can be modernized in terms of state-of-the-art technology and business.

Despite a wide range of common interests, the sociopolitical and economic conditions in the various East European regions differ significantly, and consequently the prospects for these regions vary to a great extent. A similar situation exists in Asia and South America.

- The states and companies in the central part of Eastern Europe will manage a transition within a ten-year period. Due to their history, geography, cultural and political proximity to Western Europe, Hungary, Slovakia, the Czech Republic, Poland, and Slovenia have a realistic chance of developing quickly into fully-fledged participants in the European value chain. Assuming favourable conditions, these countries could complete the transformation process by becoming formal members of the European Union (EU) within this period and achieve integration into the West European market.
- States and companies in the Baltic and the south-eastern region will be able to take the important steps towards restructuring only after political consolidation, and they will need more than ten years to complete their economic reorganization and to be fully integrated into the central European market economy.
- The CIS states (Russia, Belorus, Ukraine, and the rest) will require at least twenty to thirty years to complete the transition to a market economy that is comparable to the western structure. The conditions for development in these countries differ from those in central Eastern Europe by about the same extent that the conditions in central Eastern Europe differ from those in Western Europe. National and political consolidation is a prerequisite for stability, and planned reorganization of the CIS economy is far from completed,

largely because there is no consensus on the basic direction of economic development. Thus, badly managed state-dominated ownership is likely to prevail for a long time. It is a large task, for one thing – approximately 100 000 CIS companies need to be restructured and the related income guarantee for millions of people needs to be satisfied somehow. This task cannot be realized without the support of international investors, and this will not be forthcoming until the still dominant defence industry begins to convert its 'swords into ploughshares'.

- China, the enormous region that always has dominated Asia in terms of population and territory will, as experts see it, dominate economically and culturally by the year 2015. But China has a long way to go – the communist country is still trying to figure out how Hong Kong can be meaningfully integrated into its system in 1997. Yet, China is open regarding how the economy as a whole might develop in terms of time and direction, and it seems fairly certain that China will follow the approach taken by Korea, Taiwan, and Hong Kong.
- Mexico has long been a partner of the USA, but it is more often on the receiving end now that NAFTA has become a reality. Assembly plants in Mexico, called 'maquiladoras', have in the past added only marginal value to products that were then re-imported into the United States. Now, with NAFTA, the Mexican work force can be used in a way that adds more economic value and that also helps to create more social stability and a generally higher standard of living.

Due to this situation of vast regional differences, the planning of active new investments in emerging markets cannot follow a standardized approach. Rather, the development of strategies requires a detailed understanding of the traditions and political forces within the countries, of the structure and functional approach of companies based in those countries, and of the characteristics of the people who manage and work for them. For example, western investors initiating an East European or Chinese venture find many weaknesses in the economy that result from long-term state control, such as:

- *Underdeveloped company functions*
  - Inadequate national sales networks and weak distribution channels in and out of the countries hinder sales activities.
  - Effective supply management is non-existent; however, a storage mentality with an enhanced capability to 'organize' anything is highly developed.
  - Controlling functions are hardly known and, where these functions are implemented, the employees lack experience in managing profitability.
  - Financial officers do not understand key facets of the market economy, such as the need for capital supply and the pressure to maintain liquidity.
  - A strategic management orientation to markets and competition is not in place.

- *Lack of markets and market relations*
  - The eastern markets have collapsed, including the most significant Russian market. In China, markets are yet to be developed.
  - The old, centrally-orientated East European distribution channels have been dismantled, whereas in China they have not yet been built (except for certain areas along the coast).
  - Due to old state-controlled monopolies, existing direct relationships with western customers are few and far between.

- *Obsolete technology*
  - Technically obsolete machinery and plants with an average age of more than twenty years are the norm, and cannot be efficiently utilized.
  - Low capacity utilization characterizes those manufacturing plants that are modern.
  - An underdeveloped infrastructure creates other inefficiencies in such areas as communication and trans-

port, which require excessive amounts of time and money.
- In China, regions in the southern free trade zones are already highly developed; however, there are vast regions without significant manufacturing enterprises at all, and state-owned companies prevail in those areas.

- *Insufficient customer orientation and motivation of employees*
  - A lack of experience with market-orientated product development, cost-efficient manufacturing, or profitable sales, and a lack of familiarity with performance-based compensation are some of the reasons for low activity and creativity among employees.
  - Insufficient direct communication with customers, within project teams or with international partners, has resulted in weak communication skills such as inability to speak foreign languages and poor problem definition and decision-making. In China, a different mode of thinking – often referred to as the 'Asian mentality' – creates further barriers to effective direct communication with western counterparts.
  - Other manifestations of the socialistic way of life – such as having lengthy private telephone conversations in the office or going shopping during work hours have been due to the economy of constant shortage of communication tools and consumer goods.

- *Lack of management experience*
  - In Eastern Europe, political entities have been responsible for all of the major economic decisions for about forty years, and consequently top managers greatly lack market experience and do not have a strong orientation to profitability. In China, things are different – companies are on average smaller and less complex than those in Russia and other parts of Eastern Europe and have proved to be more adaptable to western ways, even against the Chinese backdrop of rigid central planning.

— The lack of a performance-based direction, 100 per cent job security, political control of the management, and parity among executives and subordinates (including little differences in income, formal equality within the party and workers' union and election of new managers by employees) all contribute to the informal management style of East European managers. These are also reasons for a high degree of consensus being needed between manager and workers in order to make decisions.

To understand the situation better, western companies interested in co-operating with those in the East have to recognize that the rise of the Iron Curtain eliminated only a sharp administrative borderline. However, differences between weak and strong economies remain – differences between the high standard of living enjoyed by the people of Scandinavia, Germany, Austria, and Italy and the poor economies of Russia, the Baltic States, Poland, the Czech Republic, Hungary, and the former Yugoslavia were not eliminated at the same time. In many respects, the gap has even been exacerbated. This problem is not so severe in China, where the opening process has been more incremental and thus the in-flow of western influence has come as less of a shock to the population.

Westerners also need to recognize that the opening of Eastern Europe resulted in new political freedom and increased wealth for a few, but it has also had a large negative impact, hardly seen by the West. The elimination of the state-controlled economy did not generate an immediate financial boost for a large part of the population in Eastern Europe. Instead the economic situation has deteriorated. Though this development cannot be attributed to a failure of market economy, it may not be seen that way by East Europeans and may lead to significant political changes. In China, there is no indication that the post-Deng generation of leaders will be politically less conservative than those responsible for the Tiananmen Square protest. But, over the middle to long term, they are expected to be economically liberal. Insiders believe strongly that there is no way back to a planned economy. For example, 62 per cent of Hong Kong inhabitants are convinced that their region will stay open, busy, and wealthy even after July 1997 when China takes over for good.

Investment in Eastern Europe and in China cannot be compared to investment in countries in the western hemisphere, such as Mexico. The time requirements for initiating changes are even longer than in the West. The negotiations of the Rover Group on the construction of an automobile plant in Bulgaria, for example, lasted three years and, in the fourth year, were given up altogether. Similarly, negotiations on the privatization of seven Polish cigarette manufacturers took more than two years before the Polish government agreed. After the decision was made, the date for privatization was never set, mostly because of inefficient co-ordination among the many parties involved. Thus, it should not be surprising that the western cigarette manufacturer who intended to penetrate a most promising market (approximately 40 per cent of the Polish adults are smokers) decided to build seven new greenfield plants with virtually no collaboration from the already existing tobacco companies.

Yet a growing number of successful partnerships, acquisitions, and mergers proves that tangible, satisfactory results are achievable, provided there is a workable concept and appropriate preparation. Another example, that of International Papers, is impressive: In only 75 days, the company succeeded in activating a most significant investment project in Eastern Europe. The US company invested US$150 million for the acquisition of the second largest paper mill in Poland. It was further agreed that the purchaser would invest an additional US$175 million for plant modernization to improve product quality within the first five years. Thus, for a total amount of US$325 million, International Papers has succeeded in buying a company valued at an amount three to four times higher due to investments made by the Polish government.

To understand more closely the demands that need to be faced in emerging markets, investors have to take into account how different and inconsistent conditions in these markets are.

Eastern Europe

About twenty-seven succession states have developed from the original nine East European states of Albania, Bulgaria, Czechoslovakia, GDR, Yugoslavia, Poland, Rumania, Hungary, and USSR. Fifteen succession states were created within the former USSR alone; the former Czechoslovakia has been separated into the Czech and the Slovakian Republics; the former Yugoslavia has developed into seven new states. Going forward, all of these states have to be separately analysed as to their suitability for economic development.

The historical knowledge base on Eastern Europe during communist times has become obsolete to a significant degree. New forces now determine the development in each country, and entrepreneurs who intend to operate successfully in these countries have to adjust to the new conditions.

In planning for co-operation in Eastern Europe, all of the individual country deficiencies, such as in infrastructure, have to be considered in detail; and it has been found that improvident and hasty decisions create irritating and time-consuming difficulties.

The old close relationship between the Russian economy and the economies of all East European countries dominated patterns of East European work distribution and specialisation. The nature of this relationship was characterized by Russian supply of natural resources and other raw materials to the other economies and return of investment and consumer goods to the receptive USSR-market. Thus, industrial capacities were highly specialized, and the technical structures that supported this still exist. But the related market structure is gone, and it is still very difficult for manufacturers to sell their products, except in the area of fast moving consumer goods.

The fact that individual products before 1989 were produced in only one country outside Russia is an example of this difficult situation. Take buses: Hungary had the monopoly on buses – the Ikarus plants supplied almost all East European communities. Similarly, trams were only manufactured by Tatra in Prague, and specific computer hardware was only produced in the former GDR.

The intended goal for plans such as these was to build strong mutual interdependence through a high degree of manufacturing specialization. But, as a delayed consequence of the specialization of the planned economy, there exist major companies in the East which are over-configured for today's demands. Although the necessity to discharge employees, to eliminate departments that are no longer required, and to shut down entire plants has been recognized, those measures have been implemented only in some cases.

A detailed analysis conducted by a supplier to a diesel engine industry with a work force of 2500 employees suggested that two of the three existing plants be shut down and that more than 1500 employees be discharged. The company management as well as the relevant Department of Trade and Industry recognized the deplorable situation of the company and the necessity for action; however, they delayed implementation of the required actions for an indefinite time, indicating that the sociopolitical system of the country did not provide sufficient protection for the numbers of people who would become unemployed.

This vicious circle has to be broken. Even if the speed of development cannot be accelerated significantly, projects with high publicity, such as VW's activities at Czech Skoda, can bring decisive changes in both the employees' and the general population's way of thinking and pave the way for further progress. The first priority is to develop an East–West specialized production network which creates new jobs and generates new income in the East. Success along these infrastructural lines will help to attract western capital to a large extent and to build important East–West development momentum.

China

More than any other emerging market, China, with a population of 1.2 billion, represents the region most urgently in need of investment from Triad countries and particularly from Japan, one of China's closest neighbours.

China has geared up for this investment to some extent. By 1995, fourteen special economic zones had been established, where conditions are favourable for western investment. In these zones, taxes do not have to be paid before a profit has been made, and even then tariffs will be lowered. In addition, unskilled labour only costs about 50 cents per hour. So, in view of these conditions, it is not only the huge potential market that draws investors to China.

One example of an area that has attracted western capital is the Dalian region, situated north of Beijing in Manchuria, only a two-hour flight from Tokyo. What was formerly a rural area is aggressively seeking to attract new technologies that the region has been deprived of for a long time. Dalian has already attracted an amount equivalent to US$5.3 billion in foreign (mostly Japanese) and domestic capital that has been invested in numerous joint ventures. From the perspective of western partners, money is well invested in Dalian because of the leverage. Besides cheap labour in China joint ventures can profit from cheap supply of construction material for greenfield investment.

As of 1995, more than 400 companies with foreign capital, most of them joint ventures, are active in Dalian, and more than double this number are in the process of establishing business. But even more foreign investment is needed – the city of Dalian has 5 million inhabitants, but only 90 000 jobs have been created with these joint ventures, and unemployment in Dalian is still high.

Mexico

In Mexico, where more than 80 per cent of companies are small-sized businesses with fewer than 15 employees, new investment from the USA has been flowing into the country at a greater rate than in the past as a result of the establishment of NAFTA in 1993; but more is needed. Mexico's low per capita income of US$2350 is even worse than it seems, because 2 per cent of Mexico's 90 million inhabitants are earning a quarter of the total national income and two dozen companies are responsible for nearly half of the GNP. In order to prevent the very poor 20 million Mexicans from moving 'north of the border' to look for work, the USA is an investor in the Mexican economy and, so far, the investments have been successful. Even though this collapse-threatened economy has slowed down following the sharp decline of the peso in late 1994, exporters profit from a cheaper peso, and this can help reduce the high current account deficit brought about by the peso devaluation.

After NAFTA, cross-border trade with the USA has significantly increased in both directions, with a heavy emphasis on capital goods. In general, the manufacturing base in Mexico is seen as 'fairly sophisticated' while granting sensationally low labour cost (about US$1 per hour) compared to even the poorest regions of the USA. But the miracle has yet to happen.

PRIVATIZATION AND DUAL RESTRUCTURING – THE KEY TO NEW VALUE CHAIN INTERLINKAGES

After their experience with a planned economy, all East European states share an interest in making the right steps toward a market economy. Admitting foreign capital was one of the very first changes, and this was very quickly followed by the entry of new enterprises and the introduction of new competition. Most recently, countries of the former Eastern Bloc have tried to establish a stable and efficient system of independent banking. However, due to inflation and misuse of credit, they have not been successful. Also, the privatization of formerly state-owned companies in many of the East European countries is a major obstacle to the integration with economies of the West.

Eastern Europe

Privatization has been initiated in many Eastern European countries, with some success. However, privatization without fresh capital and without people with market competence and strong market connections makes little sense and creates only small effects. That is why the expected benefits are yet to come.

Despite some success by a few privatized companies, most East European companies are finding themselves with their back against the wall. They have lost in both the export markets and the home markets since the collapse of COMECON. Sales into the more saturated western markets have only proved successful with lowest price offers, which have often been followed by western competition undercutting their prices. This then leads to problems of liquidity and unemployment and ripple effects to suppliers and their competitors. As there are almost no governmental financing instruments to interrupt such a chain reaction, bankruptcies in Eastern Europe have significant international effects.

The worries of a Czech sales manager are symptomatic. He believes that his company is capable of manufacturing the best trams for Russian cities because they can operate at the low Siberian temperatures of –40°C and at expansion joints of 10 centimetres. But customers targeted in Western European communities do not have such requirements. Instead, they require low energy consumption, minimal maintenance expense, care of track berth, low noise emission, superior design. All this could be delivered out of the Czech factory only after major capital investments in new products, product technologies, and the establishment of marketing channels.

The long-term goal of manufacturing products for the world market in eastern companies also requires a significant infusion from the West of such exports as raw materials, semi-finished products, metallurgical and chemical goods and consumer goods as well as such standard industrial products as electric engines and refrigerators.

In addition, modernization and economic reorganization of the East European economies will only succeed if western investors are prepared and economically capable of transferring production and distribution of unsophisticated, low-cost products to East European manufacturers and concentrating on more specialized, high quality, consumer-orientated goods and services.

China

Compared to Eastern Europe, China is less developed in terms of industrialization. Through the special economic zones and Hong Kong, China has become a relatively open and prepared partner for western investment. For the time being, China intends to concentrate western capital in these zones and keeps investors more or less out of the rest of the country in order to create centres of industrialization. Cooperation with Japanese companies that are seeking lower-cost production sites and new markets for Japanese goods seems to be a natural complement.

State-owned companies in China are not considered as ideal partners, and privatization is not in the offing. Since earning a profit does not add to the prestige of a manager in China, no one is really interested in showing much commitment in this direction. Nevertheless, Chinese–Japanese joint ventures are thriving and so obviously satisfy the interests of both parties – Japan's need to work cost-efficiently and China's demand for capital and employment.

Mexico

The economy of Mexico has been 'married' to that of the USA for centuries now in a relationship that has always been 'for better or for worse'. And the mutual development is ongoing – in 1982, 110 000 people worked in '*maquilado-*

ras'; by 1994, the figure had grown to 600 000. This suggests that NAFTA continues to allow the USA to be successful in its home market and the Mexicans to attract capital and earn money.

In 1994, US exports to Mexico were growing three times as fast as those to the rest of the world. Mexicans consume more US products than the Japanese. Moreover, 63 per cent of the direct foreign investment in Mexico comes from the USA. All this casts a positive light on the future – Mexico, as a threshold country, was in a more advanced stage and has already developed into a partner that the others still aspire to grow up to be; the potential for future growth is considerable.

TRIAD CAPITAL FACILITATES ACCESS TO WORLD MARKETS

New patterns of division of labour and specialization in Europe cannot be realized in one day. The same applies to conditions in China and even in Mexico. A process of economic change over several years is expected in order to increase industrialization in emerging countries and increase de-industrialization in the Triad countries. But the need for such movement is evident: German enterprises have to take advantage of favourable production opportunities in the East to maintain their export position; the Japanese are forced to find new economies by moving production to China and South-east Asia; and Americans are banking on a combination of US know-how and the favourable cost advantages in Latin America.

Due to economic competition within the Triad, West European companies will have no other chance in the near future to develop a competitive overall European economic network other than through integrating the cost-effective East European production system and adjusting it to West European technologies and sales systems.

It is a fortunate circumstance that the strong economic need for expansion of West European industry into the low-cost countries is occurring just at a time when western investors are strongly required by Eastern Europe as it hopes to become an integrated player in the world markets. This situation is comparable to the post-war period when Germany required western capital and the highly developed economic expertise of American companies (Esso, Ford, Procter & Gamble, Coca-Cola, and so on) in order to create investment momentum, economic models, and performance standards.

On a new political basis after 1949, Germany sustained an economic recovery that lasted two decades through the effective development of new products, technologies, marketing and distribution concepts, and entrepreneurial behaviour. But Germany's success relied on the support of the western powers, whose own interests were also being served. Forward movement in the German economy is still profiting from this impetus. Comparable to post-war Germany, emerging markets strongly require competent and committed investors to achieve a similar recovery. There again seems to be attractive economic potential for all parties: for the Triad investors and for the emerging markets in their parts of the world which are ready to receive investments.

The West Europeans have no alternative for significant cost reduction other than to invest in East European countries. At the same time the East Europeans have no chance to develop an efficiently operating economy without significant capital influx from the West.

Taking the obsolete technological basis into account, emerging markets urgently require large investments. In order to overcome economic isolation, the emerging markets need more than financial and technological investments. Western investors will also have to contribute ready-to-implement business concepts and access to international markets (Figure 3.1).

The most significant problem for both the East Europeans and the Chinese is psychological and rooted in the history of past decades. One pro-western Czech manager put it this way, 'Our deeply rooted socialist thinking is our

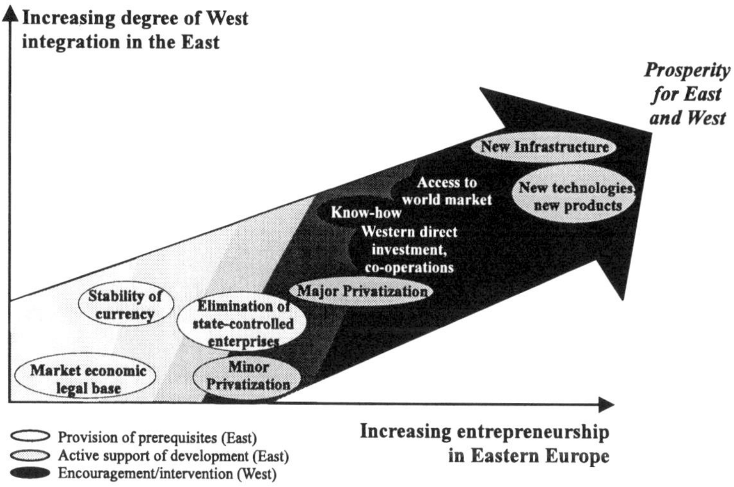

Figure 3.1 Ideal development in Eastern Europe through Western European co-operation

biggest obstacle.' It takes time to phase out old modes of thought and behavior, and this can only happen gradually.

INITIAL OPPORTUNITIES FOR TRIAD COMPANIES ARE COST-RELATED

In addition to the low factor cost an enormous market potential is ready to be exploited. Despite difficulties and investment risks, there are significant chances for Triad investors to expand and to increase the profits of their business by investing in an emerging country. For West European investors, the opportunities are particularly apparent in the central part of Eastern Europe. Moreover, the costs of raw materials, energy, and transportation are often significantly low. Moreover, in the privatization process that is occurring in Eastern Europe, companies and machines can often be acquired at favourable prices. Finally, taxes and duties in the emerging countries are often lower than in the Triad countries.

All this savings potential translates into a significant cost advantage for production in emerging markets. However, working against these cost considerations are disadvantages related to quality and productivity, and these have to be taken into account. Unreliable energy sources and unpredictability in the distribution network are other counterbalancing factors.

This, then, puts a premium on the skill of the Triad investors to apply their knowledge and techniques to the effective integration of production and supply chains in order to minimize short-term losses in manufacturing, warehousing, and transporting that are likely to result from organizational change.

There is a great opportunity for emerging markets to be supplied by western companies with consumer and investment goods manufactured cost efficiently on site, in the emerging markets themselves; but improved product quality of the goods produced in emerging markets is the primary factor for success. Through Triad investment, these countries have the chance to become efficient participants in the world market. The key tool to bring about this efficiency is Dual Restructuring. The following chapter explains why this is a powerful approach leading to win–win partnerships.

4 Dual Restructuring: Growth and Competitiveness for Companies of Industrialized Countries

Steffen Hasselwander, Carsten B. Henkel, Richard Hesch, Heinrich Seidlmeier, Erna-Maria Trixl, Michael Träm and Odo Turowski

It sounds obvious: distribution of work generates prosperity. But, in the contemporary world, this may not be the case at all. The coming decades have to prove whether this thesis is applicable for the future. There would still be uncertainty even if the basic premise is changed: prosperity is generated for all people involved if the work is distributed adequately and effectively and if value chains develop that optimally utilize the strengths of all participants. On the basis of this principle, individual countries have reached trade agreements in the past, where the main objective was to increase prosperity through an improved division of labour among the parties to the agreement and to optimize the flow of goods and services that resulted from their collaboration.

The development of such an agreement among members of the EU which took several decades seems now to take only a few years in other regions of the world. After elimination of the political split in Europe, and definitively since the 1991 agreement between the Visegrad states and the EU (establishing closer co-operation of Poland, the

Czech Republic, Slovakia, and Hungary with states of the EU), European companies can now establish new work distribution arrangements involving both western and eastern economies and increase the potential for prosperity in both areas.

A similar situation currently exists for US companies which due to the NAFTA agreement have gained access to the markets of Mexico and Central America. There is also the chance for Japan to solve some of its current problems (cost problems, stagnating markets and a strong yen) and improve its competitive position by establishing new relationships in emerging markets.

INITIAL CONSIDERATIONS: VALUE CHAIN INTERLINKAGES ARE A MUST

The economic miracle in post-war Germany was based on the transfer of American know-how in the manufacturing and service industries and the generation of completely new value chains that resulted from increased levels of German export activity. For decades, companies in all Triad countries benefited from the integration of their economy into world trade. Today, it is essential to create new linkages for profitable reallocation of value adding activities through involvement in nearby emerging countries with huge market potential. As compared to the USA and other members of the former European Community region, Germany is the leading investor in emerging countries (Figure 4.1).

Such a development as this is inevitable in the relationships among economies of the Triad and those of the emerging countries. As to Eastern Europe, decision-makers in European companies have had to expand their horizons toward the East. The potential is too great. But, in the course of implementing this new orientation, revolutionary changes in company structures and processes are required. At this stage, dual restructuring comes in. *Dual restructuring* very simply refers to the interlocking of value chains of companies in industrialized and emerging countries.

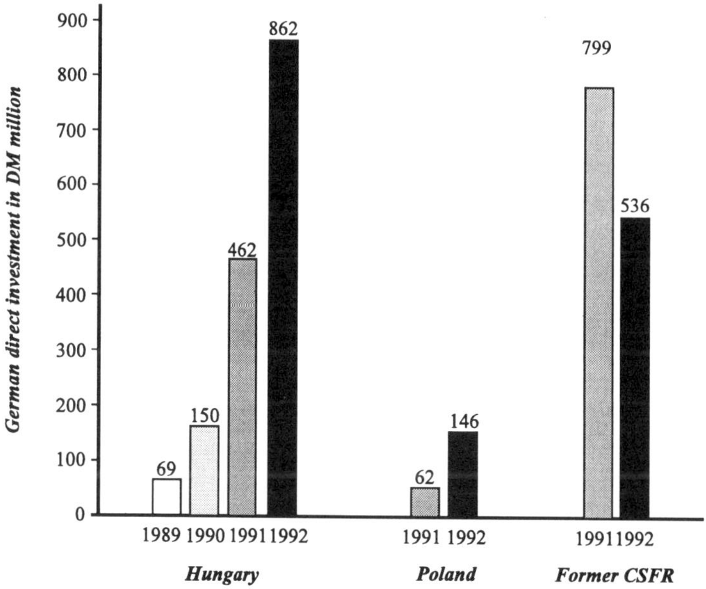

Figure 4.1 German investments in Eastern Europe

The objective of dual restructuring is to enhance the international competitiveness of both partners. Because the partners are so different, the nature of co-operative activity will be highly idiosyncratic and dependent on local conditions; however, necessary changes have to be performed by both parties involved. Neither the company in the industrialized country nor the one in the emerging country will find success in the integrated relationship without making the necessary adjustments. For example, when western companies begin to co-operate with partners in eastern economies, the following situation is typical.

- The need for change is more obvious in eastern than in western companies. For example, western investors may find their new eastern partner employs many technically skilled engineers, but inadequate levels of management and support in the purchasing, sales, and financial departments. An even greater obstacle to quick implementation and integration of new partnerships is the insufficient number of skilled service workers – in wholesale and retail, in banking and financial services, and in other important economic areas.

Differences in value structures are key problems in forging new East–West relationships; people and cultures are vastly different. That is why similar problems are also found in the alliances between US or Japanese companies and enterprises and those in other emerging countries such as Mexico or China.

- In the Triad company, change has to occur first in the way of thinking. The Triad manager needs to accept that a highly developed industrial status can only be achieved through a redistribution of work using and exploiting cheaper labour in emerging markets. A company that does not fundamentally re-orientate will be at a strategic disadvantage in the global marketplace.

Even though it would be advantageous for Western Europe to interlink value chains with Eastern Europe, the change has to go beyond this. Already, the USA and Japan have a competitive advantage in such key technologies as microelectronics, telecommunications and biotechnology, and this endangers the market share held by West European high-tech suppliers. Such suppliers have not seen the need for economic renewal.

The existing status quo mentality and the resulting inflexibility in many West European countries have to be eliminated. It is caused by a wide range of interest groups that are opposed to making the technological and organizational changes that are required. In order to improve competitiveness, the modernization of companies over the next few years must be based on dual restructuring driven by the needs for new relationships. West European companies will further establish and develop their businesses in various parts of Eastern Europe and integrate them into their European alliance in order to maintain their position in global competition. The potential for sales increase in the growing eastern markets is behind the imperative to internationalize further the western companies and their staffs. Consideration suggests that this is the only possible approach.

The same need for action exists in most Japanese and American companies which operate in global industries. The chances of significant cost reductions combined with the penetration of fast growing markets should be pursued.

STRATEGIC DECISION-MAKING: TOWARDS CO-OPERATION WITH EMERGING COUNTRIES

Companies which assume that only the opening of countries close to the Triad will develop new sales and supply markets have heavily underestimated the strategic relevance of countries in other areas, and they will probably lose out to their competitors over time.

For a European, American, or Japanese company, the magnitude of the changes required to align with companies in emerging countries varies depending on the distribution of strengths and weaknesses. This creates opportunities but also risks that increase the necessity to take action.

- Opportunities are provided for companies which already have experience in successfully developing new markets or which have established contacts in countries whose borders are currently open. This experience can be used effectively and can significantly accelerate successful entry into new markets (Figure 4.2).
- Existing weaknesses in certain western industries, such as the German machine tool industry, make it even more imperative that companies recognize the risks from newly forming sources of competition and take strategic action before their competitive position decays completely. The risk will intensify for a hesitating company when its direct competitors recognize the new international cost and market opportunities and move to improve their competitive position.

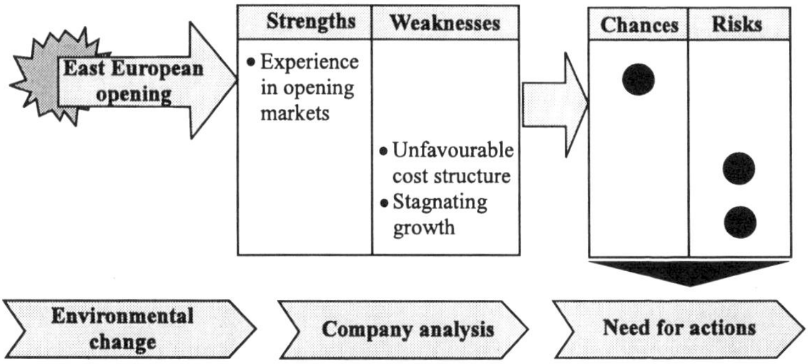

Figure 4.2 Successful market entry

What strategy should be pursued by companies in view of the opening of emerging countries such as China, Mexico, or those in Eastern Europe?

The Western–Eastern Europe combination can serve as an example of the methodology that companies can use to identify the need for action. In addition, it can be used to assess how the opportunities can be most efficiently realized by companies in the emerging countries. The methodology is fully transferable, provided it is adjusted to the specific requirements of a particular situation.

The first thing is to identify the extent to which the opening of Eastern Europe impacts upon the competitive dynamics of the relevant industry. Will there be new competitors? What activities will the competitors pursue? How fast do we have to respond to build on our strengths and eliminate our weaknesses?

Against this background, companies need to answer the question: What are the opportunities and risks that are created by this development?

- An individual opportunity/risk profile is an essential prerequisite for reviewing the company strategy and facilitating the selection of promising strategic options.
- Further prerequisites for a strategic decision are analyses of industries, markets and competitors, and potential solutions to key problems. This includes a continuous

search for niches and market gaps that promise continuing success.

The framework for these analyses and the selection of alternatives are defined by the strategic targets that are established by senior management for the company as a whole, or for an individual Strategic Business Unit (SBU), to respond to the new market opening. Instead of an isolated optimization of one individual SBU, integrated alternatives have to be developed to realize the opportunities and avoid possible risks. The example of a fictitious company – Machinery Inc. – should serve to clarify the decision-making process as well as to illustrate the inevitability of involvement in the East for many West European companies.

Machinery Inc. produces and distributes special machinery worldwide. The scenario assumes an increasingly unfavourable position: Due to the fact that the company maintains production in only one location, Machinery Inc. is confronted with an increasing competitive disadvantage in its Strategic Business Unit 2 (SBU 2). This includes cost disadvantages and currency risks. Additionally, many markets are saturated, and this saturation hinders the company in achieving its targeted level of growth without entering into cut-throat competition. The shareholder value of Machinery Inc. is also under considerable pressure.

The opening of Eastern Europe provides Machinery Inc. with a new range of strategic targets. Using the competent human resources that are available in Eastern Europe, the solid manufacturing know-how, and the existing machining capacities, the cost position of Machinery Inc. can be significantly improved. But the manufacturing strategy has to be reconsidered: is the outsourcing of complete manufacturing stages to a partner with significantly lower factor cost in Eastern Europe an alternative for Machinery Inc. or not? One thing certain is that the vertical integration of the German location has to be reduced. Thus, a second location at an East European partner facility would be advantageous. Depending on the degree of integration required, the manufacturing of parts and components could be outsourced. But, in this case, the partner should be responsible for the manufacturing of total systems. For reasons of market development, it can be appropriate later to have complete products independently manufactured in Eastern Europe or to relocate the final assembly. In a following phase marketing can be added with either a product-related and/or regionally organized sales force.

Just as the company's manufacturing strategy needs to be examined to determine adjustments to the new prerequisites, the sourcing strategy has to be reviewed. Up to this time Machinery Inc. has purchased the parts and components globally, but has excluded Eastern Europe from consideration. This will change in the future as many East European suppliers are capable of producing the required purchased parts. As many parts as possible should be manufactured by the partner company. Using this approach, the number of suppliers should be reduced drastically. It is also possible and appropriate in the plans for supplier reduction to transfer the responsibility for complete systems to the selected suppliers. This can be initiated at low risk with an already closely integrated partner.

Not only purchasing and production are affected by the change in the value chain. The marketing strategy has also to be adjusted – the SBU has to consider the advantages of a market entry into Eastern Europe and to develop implementation concepts.

Marketing, however, is only necessary as the new functional strategies of the company come into play. Assume for example that SBU2 of Machinery Inc. identifies a high demand for its special machinery in Eastern Europe but finds that the market is not yet profitable because the interested customers do not have sufficient hard currency. Until purchasing power has been established, market share can be gained through barter-trade which requires an East European partner to take over selected value-adding production steps. The produced parts could be transferred to Germany for final assembly or complete products could be produced and assembled in Eastern Europe. In correspondence with the local demand, production has to be distributed to different locations in order to generate sufficient value for exchange. Some multinational companies have already succeeded in entering the East European markets using this barter approach to market development without being confronted with any currency problems. A company-wide barter-trade can therefore be used to solve or eliminate currency problems for countries like China and Mexico.

In addition to the market development, the company has to be active in penetrating the market. Initially, the SBU is controlled from the German location. It has to be decided, however, whether a product-orientated or market-orientated sales organization is preferred, and even mixed forms are possible. In this framework, the East European partner may later take over the complete responsibility for a total East European market. If this strategy is chosen, however, the necessary support (in terms of training and resources) must be provided to develop an effective East European marketing force.

If all of this is successful and if the East European target company becomes closely integrated into the company through interlocking the value chain, product and possibly SBU responsibility can be transferred. The newly established SBU3 could eventually take over responsibility for market development in Eastern Europe, and all products would be produced there.

Another step may be to analyse opportunities and risks in geographically remote emerging countries. Depending on the market position and market potential of American and Canadian markets, parts manufacturing and/or final assembly of selected products could be jointly executed with a Mexican partner. Advantages from a manufacturing cost standpoint and access to other American markets have to be analysed in detail and the associated risks evaluated (Figure 4.3). A significant advantage to Machinery Inc. should come from reducing the potential impact of currency risk (as was experienced during the dramatic sales drop in the American market in the mid 1990s that was

SBU	Product	Western Europe	Eastern Europe	North America	Far East	Near East	Africa	South America
1	P1	●	●					
1	P2	●		●		●		●
2	P3	●		●				
2	P4	●	●					
3	P5		●				●	
3	P6	●	●		●		●	●
3	P7		●				●	

(Markets; SBU 3: Production in the East)

Figure 4.3 Product/market strategy for seven products

caused by the devaluation of the US$) and easing the impacts of future currency fluctuations.

It should, however, be indicated that Machinery Inc. does not have sufficient resources to pursue all of the geographical options at the same time. Thus, some concentration is required in order to complete the first step. This could then be followed by an extension of its business activities into, for example, Mexico as has been suggested.

In consideration of the opportunities in East Europe, there are several options for meeting the basic strategic requirements, but they contribute to the improvement of competitiveness in different ways.

- Option 1 is the opportunity of operating basically in the same way as before, that is, in global markets by means of a pure export strategy and leaving both manufacture and assembly in Germany with global sourcing for all parts required. Eastern countries would be considered as part of the global sourcing strategy. Low prices for some purchased parts would be one advantage of this option. The disadvantages, however, are that imports could be paid for only by a few customers in Eastern Europe, and the manufacturing cost of the German location would grow increasingly unfavourable as compared to the global competition. Moreover, this option cannot solve the problems from exchange rate parities and related drops in sales. Competitors co-operating with Mexican partners will take over the lost market shares of Machinery Inc., which had not only failed to develop new markets but had also lost the important US market.

- Option 2 would provide a pure export strategy for marketing and global sourcing. In addition, part of the production would be relocated into a low-cost European country, such as Ireland. The lower factor cost compared to Germany is advantageous, but this advantage would be eroded in the near future. Other shortfalls are that, due to missing buying power, countries in Eastern Europe and in Central and South America cannot effectively be penetrated with the export strategy; and cost advantages could not be realized efficiently. Again, this option does not provide any potential solutions to the currency problem, and existing market opportunities are not pursued.
- Option 3 aims at the relocation of a significant part of production to Eastern Europe and provides for entering a value chain partnership with an East European company. Production activities and marketing for Eastern Europe are integrated in one location. Significant cost advantages can be realized through the local creation of production value in Eastern Europe. At the same time, the export opportunities for these countries increase. Another advantage is the opportunity to exploit the favourable sources of supply in Eastern Europe.

Through the close relationship with the East European partner and the production location, this is more efficient than a common sourcing strategy; and significant reduction in logistics cost and time are to be expected. Then, as soon as the engagement with the East European partner has been initiated and sufficient management capacity is available in the headquarters, an appropriate partner can be sought in Mexico, making use of the experience gained in Eastern Europe. In addition to realizing the advantages of factor cost and market access, the currency problems can be diminished and the American market can be supplied competitively. The primary advantage of this third option may be found in the coordinated adjustment of various company activities to the phased pursuit of opportunities in the East, then in Mexico, and in the realization of as many synergy potentials as possible in the relationship with the partner company.

All three alternatives are screened in a benefit/value analysis against different criteria; and, even if the criteria are not weighted, the preferred alternative is identified by ranking (Figure 4.4).

		Option ①	Option ②	Option ③
• **Marketing/Sales**	Weighing	Export	In and external Barter/trade export if required	Export
— New market	4	◑	●	◑
— Demand	5	●	●	●
— Yield	5	○	●	○
• **Production**	Weighing	Production/ assembly in Germany	Production in Eastern Europe and Germany	Production in Germany and Ireland
— Cost position	5	○	●	◑
— Employee qualification	4	●	●	◑
— Logistics between production locations	2	●	◑	◑
— Quality	4	●	◑	◑
• **Purchasing**	Weighing	Global	in the East and globally	Global with focus EU
— Logistics	3	◑	◑	◑
— Terms	4	◑	●	●
— Quality of purchased parts	4	◑	◑	◑
		◕	●	◑
		Rank 2	**Rank 1**	**Rank 3**

● Completely fulfilled
○ Unfulfilled

Figure 4.4 Identification of preferred option

When all risks have been considered, and when the entrepreneurial decision has been made to pursue all opportunities presented by the opening of the East and Mexico through strategic adjustment of company activities, the most difficult step is taken: implementing the selected strategy. Successful implementation requires more than just the selection of some new suppliers or a new sales partner. Implementation must be based on the careful selection of a strategic business area for relocation, one that has the necessary development potential. This must then be followed by exploitation of cost and market opportunities, identification of the most appropriate form of co-operation, selection of an eastern target company, and finally management of the day-to-day challenges presented by restructuring.

THE PRAGMATIC APPROACH: REALIZING OBJECTIVES THROUGH DUAL RESTRUCTURING

Dual restructuring is significantly different from traditional methods of cost reduction and reorganization: it leverages the complementary strengths of two companies. The reallocation of value-added activities is regionally reorganized.

Many companies are very uncertain about future developments and weigh the negative aspects more heavily than the positive factors. This behavior is a manifestation of strongly developed risk aversion. But in fact poor results from investing in such target countries should be blamed not on a dynamic environment, but rather on the inability to implement and react flexibly to changes.

The 'optimum' expense is difficult to determine because it is dependent on the particular circumstances in the target countries, such as the degree of prior experience with performing such analyses. It is generally the case that expense cannot be so high as to impair the chances of the engagement's success. However, this does not mean that comprehensive analyses should be performed *ad infinitum*, because it is also generally recognized that the opportunities for success decline with time.

Pursue both cost and market opportunities

Traditionally, the attractiveness of the cost and/or market opportunities provides the impetus for a company to initiate business abroad.

Many German companies complain about a poor cost situation. Although Germany has a large pool of highly skilled workers to rely on, labour in Germany is the most expensive in the world. Even prior differences in the cost of labour between Western and Eastern Germany have now been balanced through tariff negotiations since the reunification.

All countries of the Triad are threatened with the loss of competitiveness, particularly in durable consumer products and capital goods. In these areas, the Japanese and German industry portfolios are strong, and cost-efficient production is an important competitive factor. The danger of competition would increase if comparable products were increasingly offered by 'threshold countries'. But, even when German companies can improve the cost factors through value engineering and thus produce the products more competitively, the other Triad countries would increasingly face pressure.

Due to relatively small home markets, pursuit of market opportunities abroad is a must for German and Japanese companies, and they have to outperform the competition. Due to the structure of the home market in the USA, American companies do not have to rely as heavily on foreign markets. Foreign involvement of US companies is primarily market-driven in the highly developed consumer goods segment.

Depending on the industry and country involved, the initiators of a dual restructuring engagement might vary. An East European engagement by a German producer of capital goods would be primarily cost-driven due to its high local labour cost. The situation would be significantly different for a US producer of soft drinks. Production costs would not be the decisive factor, so the market could be penetrated independently of the cost advantages or disadvantages – at least in the initial phase. Market factors do play an important role, however; and the newly developed market can be supplied via exports until a critical mass is achieved. In this case, the market opportunities achievable short term, not the production cost advantages, tilt the investment decision. A separation of both effects, however, is neither possible nor adequate.

In the following example, a company is primarily driven to its dual restructuring by cost advantages, but market factors also play an important role.

- A favourable cost position is a prerequisite for the realization of market opportunities and quick response to market changes is required to maintain competitiveness. But, with the increasing involvement of western companies in the eastern markets and progressive economic developments in the East, potential cost benefits are eroded over time.
- Each cost-driven German engagement in the East advances the integration of Eastern Europe into the world economy. The value added in hard currency generates buying power in Eastern Europe which is the

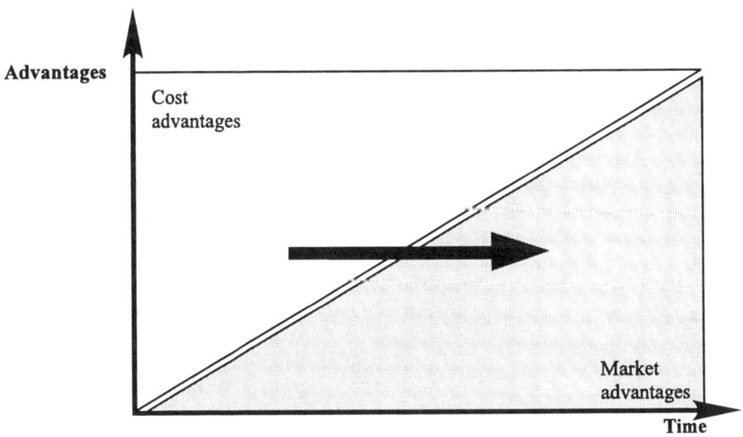

Figure 4.5 Development from cost advantages to market advantages

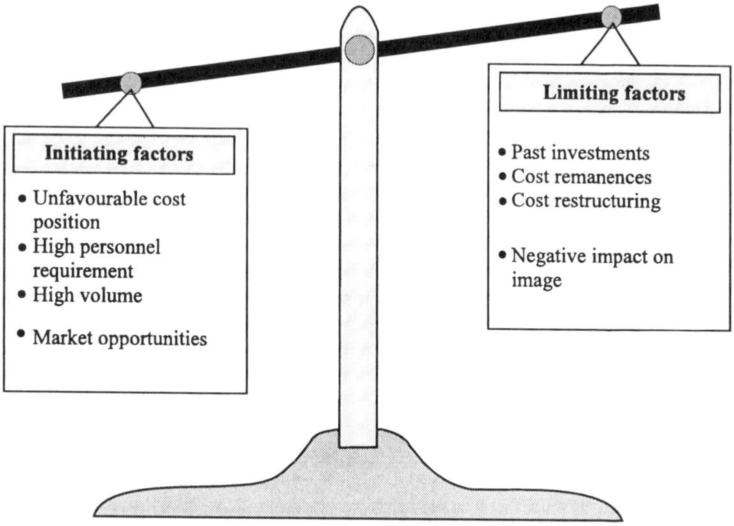

Figure 4.6 'Pro' and 'con' dual restructuring

prerequisite for enhanced market involvement and participation.

Current cost-driven engagements in the East are primarily in the capital goods industry, and the cost benefits that have been achieved there demonstrate the further potential. The initial focus of the involvement is on labour cost advantages. The labour cost differential, however, will vary by country. The impact of a single major investment might be significant in China but only marginal in Mexico.

In dual restructuring, a co-operative move into a target country is, as a rule, based on the prospect of reduced production cost, although market factors are also considered. But, in any case, the anticipated benefits need to be balanced carefully against the expense of restructuring. The following conditions contribute to a relocation decision.

- *Unfavourable cost position* A factor cost comparison for a value-adding activity with those of the best competitor might already identify cost reserves. The objective is, however, to outperform this competitor and to establish a new benchmark for the competition. Export-orientated countries need to determine whether favourable exchange rate conditions are hiding the need for cost reduction. The currently weak US$ is generating an export boom for American companies. But this advantage can turn quickly, and US companies should today identify the need to reduce costs, compare their actual costs to what is possible through dual restructuring, and act accordingly.

- *High labour intensiveness* When a company restructures to take advantage of labour cost differences, the actual improvement in cost position that it experiences will be related to the labour intensiveness of the production effort involved. It has to be taken into account that the current levels of labour intensiveness are generally the result of optimization analyses involving the local cost of capital versus the local cost of labour. At any particular time that this relationship changes locally, such as when capital cost subsidies were eliminated in Japan, a modification of the labour–capital ratio for new investments can be considered. The same applies if labour costs are very low. During dual restructuring companies always have to compare capital cost and labour cost in the target countries.
- *Sufficiently high relocation volume* Though actual cost reduction is the product of the cost advantage per unit times the number of units, it is critical that transfer costs be factored into any analysis of cost reduction. Transfer costs are the necessary costs incurred in order to eliminate a defined activity from the overall traditional value-added chain. As such costs are primarily fixed, the unit costs are reduced as relocation volume increases and relocation becomes more efficient.
- *Planned adjustment of production capacity* Two alternatives have to be differentiated:

(i) when a company plans to enlarge its production capacities due to a currently strong sales position, such as in the USA, where production capacities are fully utilized – traditionally, such a situation is an ideal trigger point for considering a new site in the target company;

(ii) when capacity utilization can more efficiently be structured by concentrating production in a more favourable cost location and shutting down existing production lines – in a case such as this, capital stock could be issued to initiate production in a target country.

- *Direct market opportunities* New market opportunities often result from dual restructuring because of improvements to market position or market share in relation to the competition. Thus, the extent to which this market potential can be realized is a driving factor.

Other factors can constrain the benefits of relocation and dual restructuring. For example, even though there may be cost advantages for an engagement in the East, the relocation, however, may still not be profitable. The following conditions argue against dual restructuring.

Situation 1

If additional costs of production (and transportation) generated through an entity that is separate from the traditional value chain exceed the benefit from relocation, the activity would not be profitable. An important component is the cost of logistics. For example, in China, even if analysis pointed to profitable production in Dalian, the huge logistics cost resulting from the lack of an appropriate infrastructure would be a decisive factor. It might be less expensive overall to support a production in the well-developed region of Shanghai. The importance of logistical considerations varies in relation to the production activity, which production steps might actually be relocated, and conditions in the target country. The proximity of America to Mexico, Germany to Eastern Europe, and Japan to China helps to reduce the impact of logistics.

Restructuring expenses in both the target and the investing country can also be a material consideration. Each company, whether it be in Eastern Europe, Central America, or China, has its own history, and initially its structure does not fit the companies in the Triad countries. The cost of creating that fit can be significant. Sometimes plants need to be renovated or replaced. In addition, there will be restructuring costs that result from creating a new management structure and introducing new programmes of quality assurance, employee training and layout planning. At the home-base, personnel also need to be retrained. Then the company needs to fund a severance plan.

Release of personnel at the home location can be handled differently in the Triad countries. In the USA, personnel can usually be released easily and inexpensively because employment agreements rarely exist except where there are unions. In Germany, it is more difficult because long-term negotiations with the workers' councils and the unions are required. Comprehensive releases are possible, although severance expenditures may be hefty. There is also the risk of reputational damage, which cannot be assessed in monetary terms. In Japan, perpetual employment is gradually being abandoned. Nippon Steel, for example, intends to reduce its administrative staff by 40 per cent and its production staff by 15 per cent through pre-retirement transfers to affiliates and suppliers.

Situation 2

Where comprehensive new investments have been made in Triad locations in people, plant, and equipment which cannot be relocated without major modification and expense, it might not make sense to move forward on a dual restructuring relationship. Is the Triad company thinking of relocating an activity with a low degree of automation, or machined parts which require highly sophisticated CAD/CAM systems? Can the local personnel be cost-effectively trained or is the work reliant on a highly skilled and educated work force? These are the kinds of questions that need to be asked. A general rule is: the decision to relocate should not only take into account the one-off transfer costs and the ongoing operating costs but also 100 per cent write-off costs. (But, as mentioned above, unused machines or machines already depreciated can help accelerate the 'pay-back' by prolonging the life of the respective machinery.)

Situation 3

Often, savings from capital dismantling are not realizable because the machines also have to be used for parts and components which should not be relocated. In the event of a relocation decision, the degree of utilization is reduced significantly. This way unit costs will go up. A real cost reduction is only achieved when the available capacities (personnel, machinery, and infrastructure) are fully reduced.

In short, the factors initiating or limiting a relocation have to be carefully analysed, and the analysis should result in the assignment of a 'net value' to each activity. Ranking of the activities to be relocated immediately due to cost considerations helps determine the final direction of dual restructuring. If and when an activity is actually relocated depends on strategic considerations.

Strategic relevance determines the individual relocation steps: detailed analysis of a product's competitive chances, in the short term and the long term, and what is required to enhance that competitiveness forms the basis for assessing the adequacy of available resources and business processes. For example, analysis of the value chain of a German furniture manufacturer revealed that product design and distribution channels are the key success factors for further growth in sales and revenue. This led to the conclusion that new distribution channels should be developed in the East (Figure 4.7) however, control should remain with the western partner.

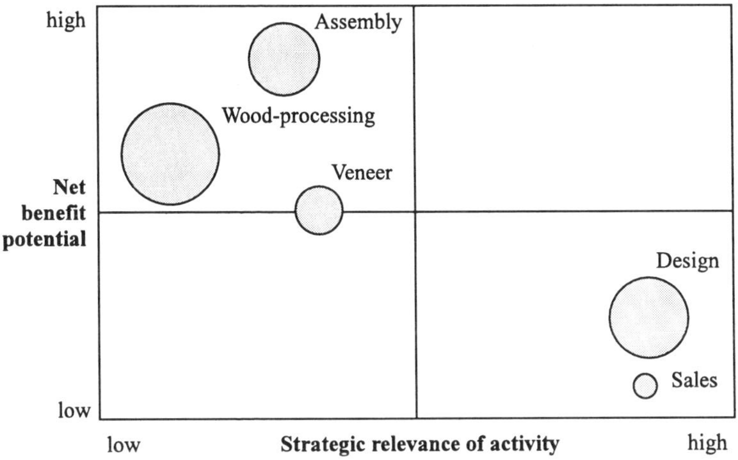

Figure 4.7 Which activities can be relocated? Example: furniture manufacturer

If a non-critical activity – one that does not significantly impact upon the total value added – is selected for relocation and the relocation is successful, then the relationship can be further extended. And, once such a non-critical activity is targeted for relocation, there are three key advantages of implementing the change, even though cost reductions might not be realized immediately:

- The learning curve is highly beneficial to the company. There is no substitute for real day to day experience of collecting data and making qualitative observations regarding product quality, delivery service, and success in restructuring the East European partner.
- If the relocation develops negatively, there is no material damage to the company.
- The restructuring expense in both the West and the East can be kept low. For example, relocation of already depreciated machines is adequate during the initial trial and transition period.

Previous experience with companies that have operated under extremely difficult conditions can provide a rough framework for an approach that may be employed over the ensuing years.

(1) Initiate the new East–West co-operation with low-intensity activities such as those that rely on a simple technology or on labour-intensive processes that require relatively low levels of experience and training.
(2) Control risk exposure by phasing in components of the processes to be transferred. The activity should not be immediately and completely relocated to the East; rather the change should be implemented in successive steps.
(3) Once the initial tests are completed with satisfactory results, the following processes may be scheduled for transfer (Figure 4.8):

    (i) manufacturing of components
    (ii) assembly of components
    (iii) manufacturing and assembly of complete product lines.

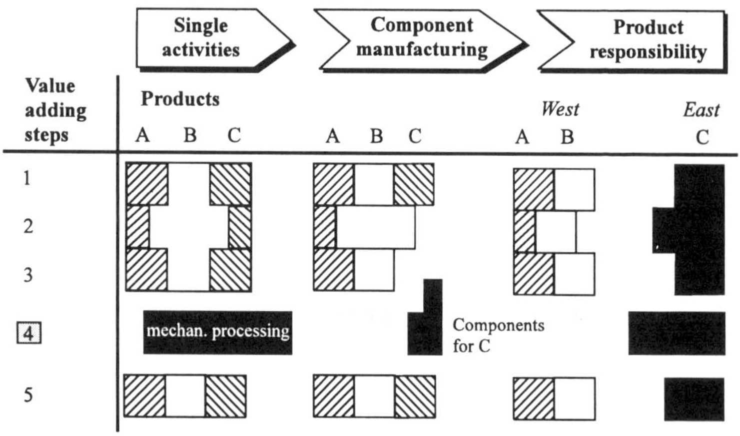

Figure 4.8 Increasing responsibility of the eastern partner with intensified co-operation

The final stage of a mature co-operation – manufacturing and assembly of complete product lines – is ideally achieved when market opportunities for sale of the product in the East first open.

Durable consumer goods and technologically unsophisticated capital goods have the best sales potential in the young eastern market. The best example of how time can shift in the life cycle of a product is the VW Beetle. This product can no longer be sold in Europe, but it is still successfully produced in Brazil. And the product has a good chance to re-establish its image as a 'people's car' in South America due to a price of about US$ 7000. Similar penetration in Eastern Europe would improve the economy and further strengthen the relationship between Eastern Europe and its western partners.

Find the best form of co-operation

After determination of the value-added steps for relocating to the emerging markets, the degree of integration has to be defined. The alternatives cover a whole spectrum, ranging from the development of a single-source partnership to the foundation of a new company in the emerging markets that may be staffed by parts of the old work force. The order of steps to full-scale integration is as follows.

(1) Establish short-term supply agreements with companies in emerging markets.
(2) Establish a supply partnership with companies in emerging markets through the creation of long-term supply agreements.
(3) Provide for franchising opportunities and/or opportunities for joint product development.
(4) Take a minority ownership share in the acquisition or joint venture.
(5) Take a majority ownership share in the acquisition or joint venture.
(6) Fully acquire a company at 100 per cent ownership, develop a 'greenfield' solution.

Within the three major emerging market blocs – Eastern Europe, Central and South America, and Asia – the scope of potential co-operative activities varies in relation to local conditions. Acquisition of land for the establishment and development of production capacities is not allowed in all countries, for example. Some production locations lack the highly skilled workers that may be required in a venture. And in many areas the political situation is unstable. Developing an adequate understanding of possible target sites can be expensive, and unplanned training needs can likewise be costly. So, in planning a co-operative relationship, the western investor may look for certain guarantees or at least want a certain degree of influence over conditions in the emerging market.

A medium-sized company in the steel industry, however, recently proved that this decision-making is not as difficult as it sounds. In relocating part of its production, the company was driven by cost reasons to look for an appropriate partner in Eastern Europe. After a detailed analysis and the subsequent rejection of several candidates due to inappropriate location, size, resources, and the like, three candidate companies were shortlisted. The decision took into account the appropriate degree of western influence and control. It was important that the target company should be able to produce cost-efficiently and respond to changes in customer requirements at any time. Such an ownership position was not legally permissible with two of the three candidates, thus only one company was left. In the final analysis, the investor decided on a joint venture with another western company which also wanted to relocate a part of its production, and the venture acquired 95 per cent of the capital of the target company in the East.

For such a decision, the following general rule applies: the higher the strategic relevance of the value-added step to be relocated, the greater the degree of influence and control that the western entity should have over the target company. If the emerging market is solely to be used as a favourable source of supply for unsophisticated and/or non-critical parts, supply agreements without any further financial commitment may be all that is necessary. However, should the target company be fully integrated into the value chain in order to assure the competitive position over the long term. The investing company has to gain control over the activities of the partner in the emerging country.

Back to the example of the steel company: meeting quality standards was critical for the company's success; thus the relationship was of strategic relevance. A supply agreement in this situation would not provide adequate protection because the company would lose control over the quality of parts. In order to move forward, the western company had to ensure its voice in management by becoming a majority owner.

Differences among individual countries in the emerging markets also have to be taken into account. Recently, there have been complaints from companies investing in China that they have not been able to realize the projected levels of earnings. In some cases the business world has been shocked when, after technology and know-how had been invested in the Chinese joint venture, the western partner was considered to be no longer required, and the joint venture products soon faced competition from less expensive copies produced by the Chinese parent company. Clearly, the western partners have not obtained sufficient protection for the technology transfers, and experience shows that it takes a long time to develop the contractual frameworks in which European and US investors would find adequate safeguards.

With South American and East European partners, contracts are regarded as binding; but, with Chinese partners, it is likely that one will find important discrepancies in the contracts. Thus, it is becoming increasingly important to factor in basic controls even in simple supplier relationships.

Experienced global players learned lessons early on. A great number of companies completely avoid activities in the East if they do not get a certain amount of control. Asea Brown Boveri (ABB) for example, rarely takes a minority position in Eastern Europe. As soon as the corporation gains control over the target company, ABB immediately implements a controlling and quality assurance system meeting western standards. Until and unless this control is in place and cost-driving activities have been restructured, ABB does not start production.

In China, ABB expands primarily through joint ventures. Alexis Fries, President and chief executive of ABB Asia Pacific Ltd, recently noted, 'To start joint ventures loosely, without really understanding what you do and failing to understand each other, is doomed to fail.' The important features are: strict control, excellent training, a high degree of management accountability, and meaningful systems for incentives and sanctions.

Be selective in finding an emerging market partner

Assuming that development of a new market (and not cost-efficient production) is the key objective of the western investor, the attractiveness of a local partner is found in the market position and the network of customer contacts. If these aspects are favourable, the western partner will generally seek to develop the market quickly because there is a time-related advantage over companies which may be pursuing a similar expansion course but without a local partner.

The three regional blocs of emerging markets have different appeals to western investors. Generally, there are two key motives to the investors: (1) cost reduction in the worldwide value-adding process, and (2) increased market penetration. Against this backdrop, Eastern Europe is attractive to those in traditional manufacturing industries and mainly for cost reasons.

Companies based in the USA are looking to the south for reasons of cost reduction and market penetration. Mexico, for example, particularly after NAFTA, is regarded as an exceptional location for finding reduced labour cost and thus for adding production value. In the MERCOSUR countries – including Brazil, Uruguay, Paraguay and Argentina – a better balance between cost factors and market penetration is provided. On the one hand, a sufficient low-cost work force is available (although it is more expensive than that in China or Russia). On the other hand, relocation to this economic region guarantees an expansion into MERCOSUR without customs or tariff barriers.

Labour is cheaper in China, but the strong historical, cultural, and psychological differences increase the difficulty of finding a low-cost location. Thus, most companies adopt the position of a market conqueror and aim at tapping the huge market potential. As the *Financial Times* commented, 'More than anything, it is China's potential that drags hungry companies in droves.' According to the Business Coalition for US–China trade, the potential market looks like this: $40 billion over the next 20 years for aerospace, $90 billion over the next 7 years for power generation equipment, $29 billion over the next 5 years for telecommunications, $18.2 billion over the next 3 years for oil field and gas machinery, and $4.3 billion over the next 8 years for computers.

It is a similar situation, although not nearly as dramatic, in the other Asian countries. Any savings in labour cost may be lost through excessive logistics cost, but the market potential of the ASEAN-countries is considered compelling. Avery Dennison, a $2.6 billion California-based maker of consumer product labels, has established a plant in Indonesia. The Indonesian market in itself is too small, but the possibility of an unhampered penetration of the ASEAN-countries is reportedly the key factor in the involvement there.

In order for Eastern Europe to gain attractiveness from a marketing perspective, an East European distribution network needs to be developed. Large market shares are in the offing for those companies which recognize the immediate need for action. The required investments are of a strategic nature and are calculated as such.

If the approach is purely market-orientated, there are no major expenses associated with dual restructuring – neither by the investing nor by the target company – because the traditional business areas remain largely unchanged. In simple terms, a new regional division may be implemented in addition to the existing divisions, but only the operating areas of logistics and production planning are affected by the emerging market activity. The adjustment requirement is marginal: value added activities are hardly changed and a pure export strategy is often pursued.

The situation completely changes for a resource-induced engagement in the emerging markets, where for the first time local production is factored into the manufacturing process. The interest in developing such a capability may not simply be that the western partner has reached its production capacity. Rather, it may be that its cost reduction limits have been reached, and future competitiveness may no longer be a given. In the East, machine capacities and underutilized human resources are to a large extent still available.

Analysis of complementary strengths and weaknesses is a difficult but highly important building block for a successful East–West partnership, because as soon as international boundaries are crossed environmental complexity and the need for organizational changes increase significantly.

Methodologically, two steps have to be pursued in order to identify potential partners:

(1) write a description of the activities that will be relocated in the value-added portfolio and a list of the net benefits and strategic gains that will result from the relocation;
(2) determine, or estimate, the probable changes to the cost position of the entire value chain and to the strategic resource position that will be achieved by the engagement. The development potential is dependent on the scope of factors present in the company environment as well as the concrete situation of the target company being considered. Note that this assessment of benefits generated from the reconfiguration of the value chain under varying conditions can be costly.

As suggested, taking the individual country-related criteria into account is essential in the search for a location, although the importance of such information depends on the intensity of the co-operation. The more extensive the nature of the co-operative relationship (along the (1)–(6) spectrum outlined above) and the greater the strategic relevance of the activity to be relocated, the more comprehensive information is needed. In order for this to be meaningful, however, the company considering dual restructuring should be open to all possibilities.

To go back to the West–East European example: what all East European countries have in common is that currently the hourly wages are on average about 5 per cent of the German level. Here, the following rule of thumb may be applied: the farther you go from the West European market, the lower the wage level is. In addition, western investors will find a large number of technically skilled workers and engineers in the East European markets. Initially, the significant and achievable labour cost advantages are partly reduced through the productivity gap; but, over the long term, such a gap should not to be considered as a risk, but as an opportunity to provide additional cost reductions following successful restructuring. Thus, the future labour cost increase in the East will be more than made up through productivity gains; and, in view of certain existing differentials between markets in Eastern and Western Europe, there is ample room for labour costs to rise in certain countries for some years before an adverse effect is felt.

To improve productivity, major new investment in machinery and facilities is not required. Due to the partly chaotic work organization in East European companies, a reorganization of production processes is sufficient to generate significant effects on productivity.

The entrepreneur who is ready to invest has to plan for significant restructuring in order to raise the productivity of the South American industry to the level of European or American industry. Using the automotive industry as an example, one can observe that the Brazilian productivity rate is 10 per cent less than that in Western Europe, and the productivity level of the Argentine automotive industry is another 10 to 20 per cent less than that in Brazil. This productivity differential, however, is compensated for by a lower labour cost basis compared to Europe.

As the production factor 'labour' is impossible to move to a large extent (otherwise, labour costs would level worldwide), a company gaining a labour benefit from its location in the emerging markets has to take into account the cost of logistics.

- **Logistics efforts will increase** – qualitatively and quantitatively:
  - *qualitative* The infrastructural components must be in place to transport goods from A to B. This can be assumed in Western Europe and adjoining countries as well as in the USA and South American countries, but the infrastructure might be a problem in countries on the edge of Eastern Europe and in some Asian regions.
  - *quantitative* The logistics cost should not meet or exceed the level of cost savings achievable through relocation:

(i) the value-added process has to enable significant cost reduction in order to benefit from the relocation;
(ii) the value-added process may not be fragmented at random;
(iii) the critical size for efficient and cost-effective logistics must be achieved;
(iv) relocation has to be within reach.

- **Cycle times will increase** – due to the relocation, it is expected that the cycle times will increase for a short period, which will affect profitability. In many companies reorganization of business processes will solve inefficiencies induced by long throughput times or low productivity.

It is generally recommended that locations in the immediate neighbourhood be considered if a cost-efficient location in the emerging markets is identified for the optimization of the overall value chain. Depending on the product characteristics and the complexity of the value delivery process, a distance of several thousand kilometres might also be adequate. Logistics cost, however, is the major limiting factor.

As indicated, finding and following the path to all potential advantages is difficult. An adequate starting point is the relocation of single and unsophisticated manufacturing processes, because significant benefits can already be achieved – particularly in industries with high labour cost – through loose alliances. But, once the relocation process is begun, the western investor begins to gain valuable experience. As valuable information is gained in the day-to-day business (especially in view of the planned intensification of the co-operation), the risks of failure are minimized. In addition, the actual business risk remains within calculable and acceptable limits, in view of the low strategic relevance of the relocated activities. For these reasons, it is obvious why, at the start of restructuring, a US company prefers to relocate the first production step to Mexico rather than to Russia – the expense of moving into Russia would be too high.

In the later stages of co-operative dual restructuring, there are many reasons to intensify the effort through closer East–West co-operation.

- At a later stage it may make sense to intensify the co-operation so that the resources that have been mobilized are prevented from becoming failed investments. In this context, the investing company should only invest into restructuring if it can exclusively realize the advantages of this activity.
- The expected advantage from the relocation of two activities is sometimes not realized in a loose co-operation because a linking activity should stay in-house for strategic reasons. If this one activity cannot be relocated it will not be efficient to relocate the others because then the small cost reduction effect will be eaten up by the logistics cost.

Therefore, intensified co-operation is necessary to secure strategically important processes.

- A closer co-operation could be useful in managing resource costs and in enhancing market competitiveness.

Depending on the selection of target country, intensification of the co-operation can take on different aspects:

- The intensification of co-operation should be a by-product of increasing integration in the partnership between the investing and the target company. The implication is that conditions in the emerging countries themselves can become major issues in the decision-making process. In this, however, there is little clarity. For example, the legal foundation for co-operation in East European reform countries is not yet stabilized, and it differs significantly from the standards in China. Many countries in emerging regions lack a continuous development plan, the political situation is unsettled, and few clear trends can be identified. Investors are frequently sur-

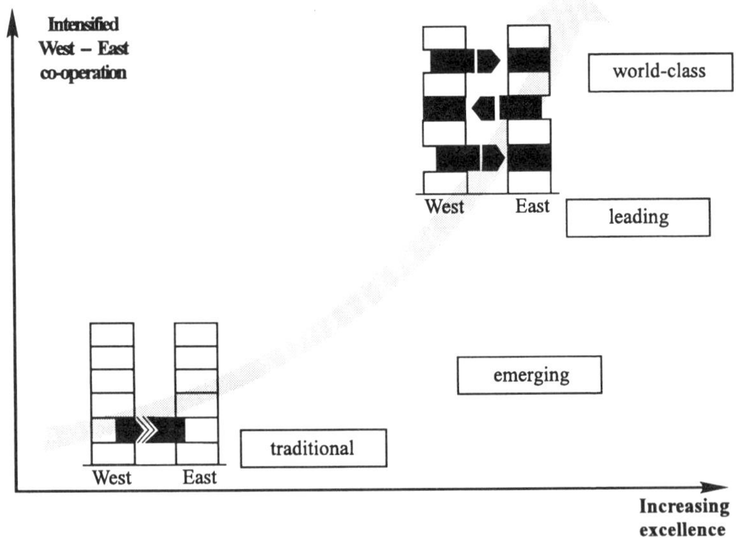

Figure 4.9 'Stages of excellence'

prised by unexpected and pointless regulations. In Eastern Europe, the situation varies with location – the more important the western investment is for the East European partner country, the more flexible the local authorities will be in granting special approvals and making special arrangements.
- In addition, the socioeconomic conditions of the individual countries have to be taken into account; however, due to inadequate and unreliable data, observations are based on general and hardly differentiating indices, such as GNP. So, in the current environment, market potential can only be roughly estimated at best.

Beyond the 'home' market, markets in neighbouring countries should also be considered to facilitate the development of bridgeheads, but the multilateral relationships are complicated too. For example, there is a greater affinity among the Baltic States than between Russia and the Ukraine. On the other hand, suddenly freed from the pressure of conformity, many former Eastern Bloc countries increasingly want to differentiate themselves from their neighbours.

- All trade barriers within the various groups in Central and South America will be eliminated eventually. In Mexico, for example, one benefits from NAFTA and the 'group of three' (Mexico, Columbia, and Venezuela). Further south, there is MERCOSUR (Argentina, Brazil, Paraguay and Uruguay).
- There are similar prerequisites within the ASEAN states, and integration with America is supported by the APEC.

A careful weighing of both short-term cost reduction effects and medium-term market effects is required to make sound investment decisions. In Eastern Europe, labour cost-related considerations point to investment in Romania, but market considerations favour Poland. The size and characteristics of achievable effects on capital returns will influence the decision for a certain country; but, in any event, management has to balance short-term cost reduction considerations and medium-term market gains in order to ensure support for defined company targets.

For the selection of the partner company, assessment of both the country and the company should be integrated with the strategic criteria established by the investing company. Generally, in preparation for the selection, the investing company develops an image of an ideal partner – as to size, competence of personnel and availability of resources.

If a whole company is to be acquired, the expected restructuring potential is of special significance. In the case of developing a supply relationship, it is the current company status that is important. Existing resources must be capable of immediately satisfying the required performance and service expectations (Figure 4.10).

The ability of a target company to satisfy all the requirements of the partner plays a key role in the development of sources in the emerging markets, and all important criteria should be analysed diligently (Figure 4.11). Such an audit in Eastern Europe or in China, for example, is more difficult to perform due to lack of adequate data. Company valuation is only relevant for the acquisition of shares or of the company as a whole.

A company which anticipates an engagement in the emerging markets has to realize that the search for a

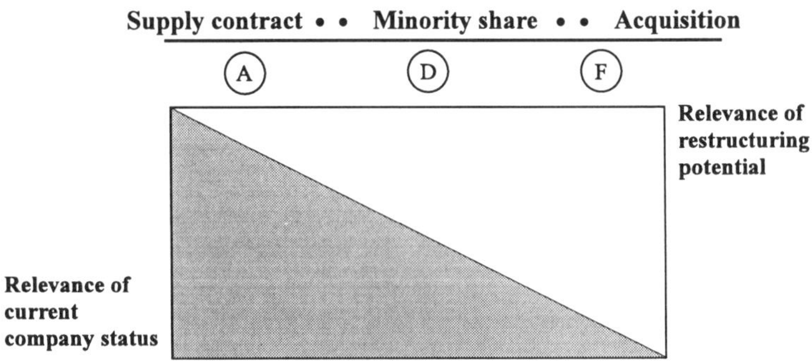

Figure 4.10 Stages of dual restructuring

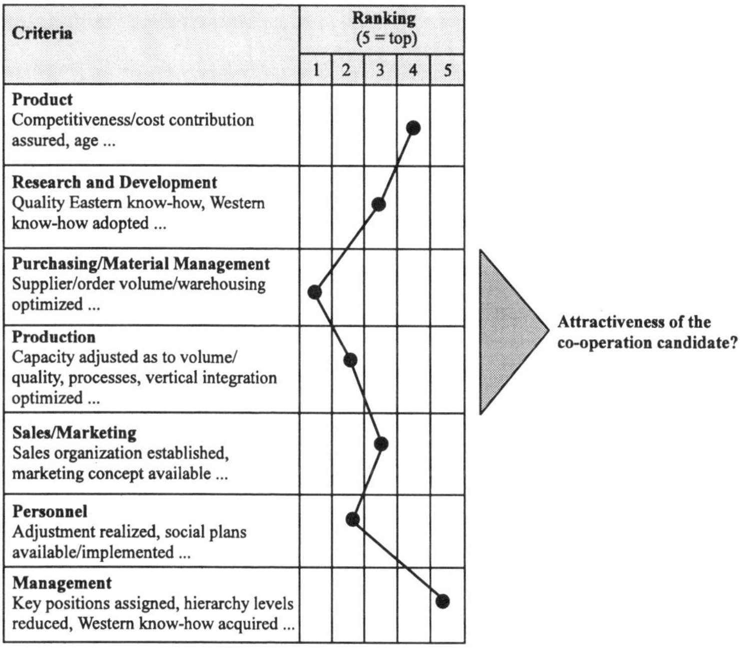

Figure 4.11 Company valuation

partner is significantly different from the identification of an acquisition candidate or a co-operation partner in the traditional industrialized countries. Here companies have considerable recent experience with mergers and acquisition. In these more stable economies, the searching company does not face major difficulties in assessing the potential partner due to similar structures, easy data availability, and clear ideas about market image. In emerging markets, the same kind of analytical approach is significantly more time consuming and not nearly as revealing. Nonetheless, it should still be possible to recognize problems and to identify barriers which need to be eliminated.

If co-operation or acquisition is pursued, a detailed analysis (see Figure 4.12) of the potential candidate and the achievable benefits may highlight some of the existing

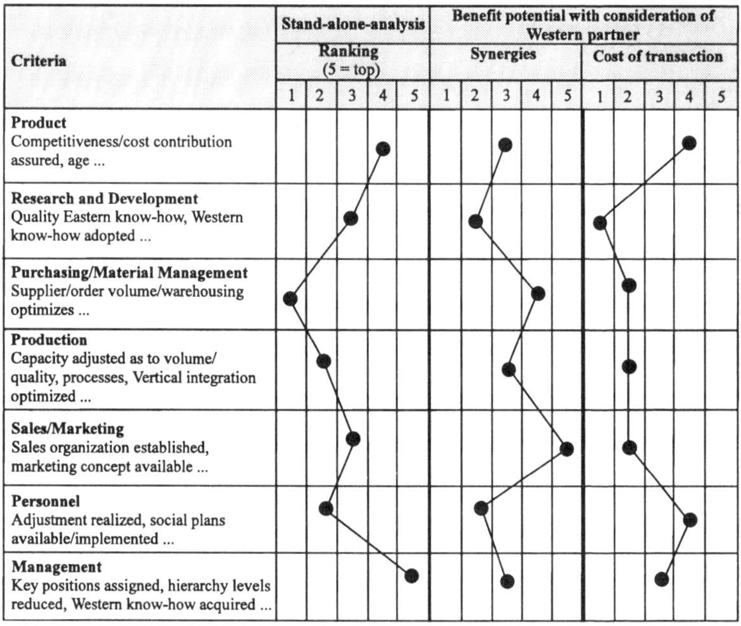

Figure 4.12 Audit of an East European company

problems. The audit of an East European company can serve as an example.

To start with, a typical combine can hardly be compared to any major Triad enterprise. As to the potential scope of activity, eastern companies are huge organizations (Figure 4.13). There is too much administration, too many hierarchical levels; lower and middle managers are not skilled in decision-making and obtaining approval for relatively unimportant decisions is time-consuming. Even companies with more than 30 000 employees are highly centralized, and there is a corresponding high degree of bureaucracy. Vertical integration of major companies reaches almost 100 per cent. In addition to manufacturing, these *kombinats* maintain social services that in the West are usually provided by local government and private enterprises (such as

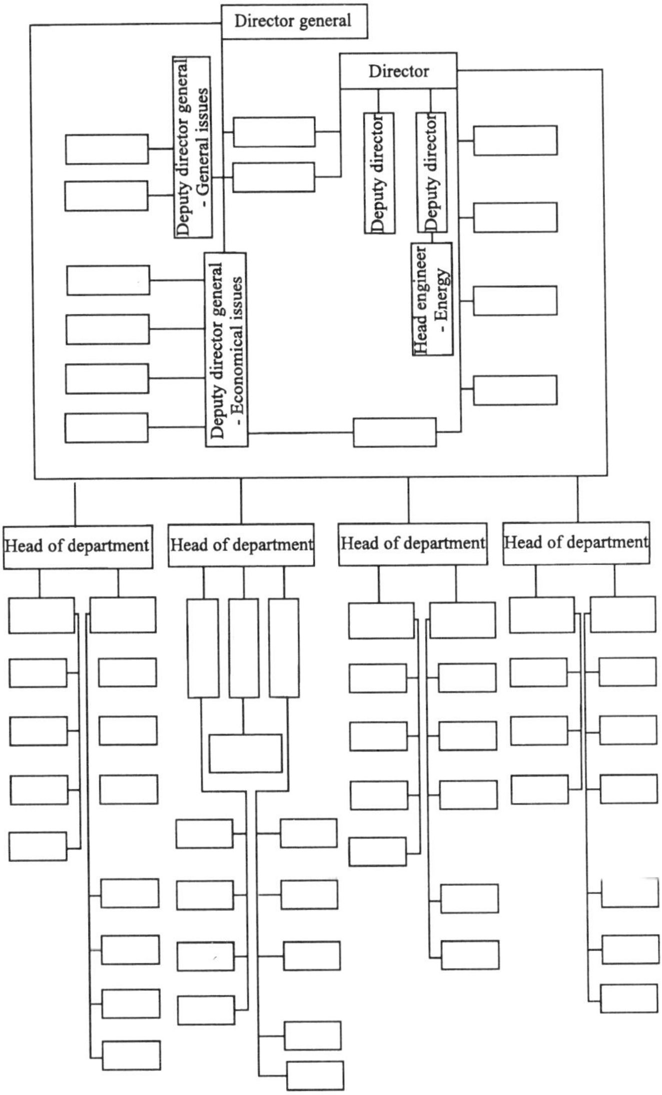

Figure 4.13 Highly complex *kombinat* structure

transportation, schools and child care centres, recreation centres, and hospitals).

An interested western company which intends to conduct an audit or to perform a valuation assessment of the potential eastern partner faces some major difficulties. Here is a description of a visit to a Russian *kombinat*:

> The key intention of our visit was to analyse the capabilities of a potential co-operation partner for a western client. From trade fairs, customer contacts, and the like, the potential candidates were already known, as were the names of the persons to contact. The company to visit was situated in the interior of Russia. It belonged to the aerospace industry and produced engines for the Iljushin and Tupolev product lines. In addition to the core products, the company produced engines and components for the Russian defence industry.
>
> Our journey from Berlin took almost 17 hours and included a two and a half hour break for changing over from the international airport in Moscow to the national airport. This period also included waiting for our Russian hosts at the destination because apparently nobody expected the Aeroflot plane to arrive punctually. Finally, eight representatives welcomed us at the airport and took us in a Toyota minivan on a one-hour drive to the only hotel in town.
>
> The next morning, the 'representative for foreign visitors' picked us up from the hotel and invited us to have breakfast. What we understood would be a light refreshment was expanded by the Russians into a two-hour meal. All attempts to discuss the real purpose of our visit were greeted by a friendly nod and a continuous refilling of our cups. Finally, the company directors entered and we could commence negotiations.
>
> The negotiations started with a thorough introduction in which our hosts depicted the history of the company and its many contributions to the Russian aerospace industry. We were expected to visit the company-owned exhibition immediately and to get acquainted with the

considerable range of merits of both the company and its employees.

Later on, the actual visit to the museum took place, which became an impressive demonstration of the history of Russian aerospace techniques and the pioneers of this industry. Our negotiations, however, had a completely different intention, aimed at the company's general appropriateness for co-operation and the specific potential for its restructuring.

During the course of our visit, we eventually met the responsible directors to whom we could address our questions. The first meetings, in a visit scheduled for three days, appeared to be very inefficient. Mostly, the Russians politely took note of our questions but answered them without specific information or detailed figures. Even questions on the current number of employees remained unanswered. The numbers provided by the directors and by the general manager differed by some 4000 employees.

The discrepancy was explained by virtue of the fact that, due to reorganization of the company, the current number of employees in the so-called 'social service' was not available. One has to keep in mind that in addition to obvious services such as a canteen and a company medical facility, a Russian company – not unlike one in China – maintains a wide range of other social services, including hospitals, sport facilities, company housing, and local transport facilities. Depending on the size and location of the company, up to 20 per cent of costs can be attributed to these 'social services.'

The companies increasingly attempt to get rid of those costs and to transfer the responsibility to the local or regional authorities but they lack the financial wherewithal to take on the responsibility. As responsibility for these activities has only partly been transferred to local authorities this fact is used as an excuse for not precisely indicating the number of employees.

Getting answers to questions on sales and to requests for the detailed information behind these indices required some persuasion. Initially, most questions about products remained unanswered on the grounds that the company was a major supplier to the defence industry. After intervention on the part of the general manager, we succeeded in getting even these questions answered. However, the questions required the approval of the company's 'security officer' who also had to approve our fax transmission to our Moscow office indicating that we wanted to change our hotel accommodation.

After the initial distrust of the directors had dissipated, however, we received the required information. In particular, the company's data on future plans was of special significance. In addition, a detailed survey on the company's planning methodology was provided in a long meeting with the finance director. As we could not find any computers other than the word processors of a few secretaries, we wondered how the planning effort was supported (in addition to the accounting and fiscal control functions).

The finance director, responsible for at least 40 000 employees, had his own planning methodology: all planning data for the next five years were displayed on large flipcharts fixed to the wall. At least twenty charts were hanging on top of each other and they were logically linked. A simple change to an individual figure caused a time-consuming rewriting of those charts, and therefore changes had not been executed for a long time. We also found evidence of 'hockey-stick planning' which is typical for eastern companies. By this method, short-term and dramatic decreases in output and sales are blamed on the economic adjustment processes of East European companies. Generally they assume that the company will quickly recover with stable growth at double-digit rates. The assessment of these data and plans in such a way that useful information can be generated from the unrealistic company figures requires a high degree of familiarity with other Russian and East European companies which provide a comparative reference point.

> Supposedly, senior management was already familiar with 'new' management tools from several seminars they had been to in western countries. But the Russians had not been very successful in the selection of those seminars – most of the money and time was spent learning about generic problems, related to integrating spirit, management, and the environment, for example. The needs of an East European company in this difficult time were not really addressed, and the Russians' understanding was completely different when it came to technical matters.
>
> After the initial distrust had disappeared, the Russians recognized that we were also experts, and we were finally allowed to gain insight into the whole manufacturing process. Even though we found halls the size of football fields and one manufacturing centre arranged next to another in diffuse semi-darkness, we gained a very positive impression of the manufacturing facilities as to machine equipment and manufacturing quality. Belonging to some extent to the defence industry, the company could claim a comparatively high level of public investment. The managers obligingly showed us some modern western numerically controlled manufacturing centres, indicating that despite politically induced western export restrictions, the Russians had succeeded in purchasing all necessary equipment.
>
> At the end of our visit, we left a list of all unanswered questions with the general manager who promised to provide us with all outstanding information; and, after several days and a few telephone calls to our Moscow colleagues, we finally received the required information.

As this example shows, unsophisticated and objective data on sales, manufacturing cost, and the number of employees are often hard to determine, and company value can only be estimated after detailed analyses. Basically, discounted cash-flow can not be calculated. Thus, the only opportunity for a potential investor is to estimate and assess an East European company on the basis of his prior experience.

The identifiable restructuring potential of a company has to be estimated as very high. What is the scope of improvement the company in the emerging market can achieve after restructuring activities by the Triad partner? A cost reduction potential of more than 20 per cent is realistic for well-structured companies. Obviously, a prerequisite is convincing management of the benefits of restructuring. Providing the same level of stringency in the activities, the savings potential in the emerging market company is two to three times higher than that.

This savings potential rests on a broad range of factors. An excessive number of employees in almost all eastern companies is the most important one, and it is followed by inefficiency and lack of motivation. In addition, it can be observed that even the best employees of an eastern company are unable to fulfil an order from start to finish according to western standards and at the same time meet both time and quality requirements. The restructuring potential, of course, does not only aim at realizing savings through personnel reductions. The introduction of lean structures and processes also generates savings and thus affects the profit situation positively.

The expected opportunity/benefit potential in such areas as cost reduction, turnaround time, or quality improvement has to be assessed in relation to the expense savings and the necessary time to implement the change.

For each value-added step of the eastern partner, the biggest improvement levers have to be identified. Global sourcing is regarded as one lever in purchasing. The consolidation of the plant layout is another – it results in a significant reduction in the production lead time. On the basis of experience, there is almost always potential to generate savings by implementing a quality assurance system.

Similar to the integration of acquired companies into the concern, the factor time plays a major role in the assessment of restructuring potential, and expenditures are often underestimated. Successful western investors claim that thorough restructuring activities in the East have to be completed after approximately one year.

For the assessment of the eastern company, an industry comparison in the East European economy is meaningful, whereas comparison to a western company would only generate ambiguous results. It is generally the case that the better the eastern partner performs compared to competition, the more successful its integration with a western partner will be. In addition, the resource base, product quality, R&D capabilities, and the technical/management know-how have to be compared to competing eastern enterprises. In order to identify whether the company is capable of performing above average, an industry average has to be determined.

The corporate culture of both partners is also taken into account. It is not sufficient to check the 'cultural fit' as is done in the acquisition by a western partner. Generally, management has to completely change its thinking, since the concept of centrally controlled structures is deeply rooted in behavior. If the western company does not succeed in convincing the eastern partner of the necessity for quick change, the realization of restructuring activities will become more difficult with time. Changing management is often the only way to achieve the required turnaround.

In China, similar, if not more severe, problems are encountered. What is common in both economic regions is the centralist pattern, but there is a completely different cultural background in China. It is increasingly the case in China that foreigners are accepted, but not perceived as useful partners. It is especially important in this atmosphere to develop a basis for confidence and to establish conformity in the expectations of both parties involved. In particular, Chinese top management cannot be removed.

The influence of local management and employees has to be taken into account in such cases. The area of influence and responsibility of a general manager of a former East European armaments plant with 40 000 employees is not comparable to that of a western manager. The eastern manager on the other hand can exercise social and political control in an environment where the *kombinat* is the only significant employer. This has to be adequately assessed when selecting a partner company. The more power management holds, the less support there is for western objectives and the more difficult it is to implement change.

Three key factors are relevant in the company audit, whether it is a Chinese, Russian, or Mexican company that has to be evaluated as to its restructuring potential:

- profit potential
- restructuring expense
- restructuring time.

An unmotivated or dominating eastern management will lengthen the restructuring time and drive up restructuring cost. The better the resource position of an eastern company, the higher the profit potential will be. These individual factors have to be assessed and then integrated to form an overall impression of the potential company.

Flexibility is required because much of the internal financial information can only be estimated. The investing company has to weigh the relevance of the three criteria. The restructuring potential of each of the eastern candidates can be identified and compared, and the company with the most favourable location and the biggest restructuring potential will finally succeed.

Manage the challenges of restructuring

If the venture is ill-prepared, the cost of restructuring a partner company in an emerging market may exceed the benefits. Indeed, this is the main reason why, in some instances, interlocking value chains with companies in emerging markets turns out not to be worthwhile. Thus, the restructuring requirements and related costs have to be estimated as realistically and reliably as possible ahead of time, and at the same time the co-operation with the partner in the emerging market has to be organized in such a way that the restructuring requirements remain as low as possible.

Although interlocking value chains is a paramount issue across the Triad, requirements for dual structuring and restructuring will vary greatly from region to region. Between the three regions, the situation is most challenging in Eastern Europe because of three factors:

- huge company size and high level of integration, both horizontally and vertically;
- the intricate system of COMECON and its sudden collapse;
- an economic and ideological system that dramatically changed practically overnight, providing high degrees of freedom but also instability.

Taking advantage of the favourable factor costs without getting mired in endless and expensive restructuring (which would more than offset any advantage) requires some skillful manoeuvring in light of the complexity of East European companies.

In many cases, the organizational structure can hardly be understood by outsiders, and the number of hierarchical levels and interfaces increases the complexity of processes. The newcomer to Eastern Europe tends to interpret the fragmentation of activities as a lack of personal responsibility and attributes it to people's mindset. The shortcomings, however, are more related to the nature of the economic system than to people's mentality.

Unreliable deliveries, for example, are often caused by a machine that is idle due to the delayed provision of necessary spare parts. If a machine breaks down, the machine operator informs the foreman who passes on the spare part requirement to his superior, who for his part communicates it to the head of materials management. Another two hierarchical levels are involved until the request finally reaches an employee who can identify whether the required spare part is in stock or can be produced in-house or whether it must be purchased externally. If one link in the chain fails to pass on the information, the respective machine is out of operation for perhaps four days instead of two days.

The westerner who is confronted with such a procedure for the first time wonders why the machine operator does not immediately get the spare part from stock, but the East European supplier will explain that it is against common practice not to involve superiors. What at first sight looks like lack of initiative is instead an attempt to observe the regulations (which are not subject to discussion in a country which has always been ruled in an authoritarian way). This in particular applies to the large, unwieldy companies which, in contrast to smaller entities, do not encourage individual initiative among employees.

The high degree of worker specialization, based on extremely narrow bands of responsibility, is the result of a highly developed plan of division of labour which effectively enabled mass production. In work preparation, one engineer is responsible for scheduling and lot size planning of precisely defined tools. Then there are specialized machine operators. A combination of small, medium, and large work pieces with a mix of conventional and specialized machines may result in nine different operators for one function, such as lathing.

The highly developed principles of labour division apply to all operating areas and continue in administration. In the overhead areas, specialization is increased in direct relationship to the number of productive employees. The number of bookkeepers will increase with the number of employees in the operating areas. In addition to poor data processing support, the high degree of vertical integration which is typical for East European companies is another reason for the large workforce. The permanent deficiencies in supply caused the companies to extend their activities beyond core businesses to include, for example, the production of spare parts for their machines.

As long as capacities were fully utilized, the large number of employees was not a problem. Yet, as the economic situation deteriorated, and particularly following the collapse of COMECON, idle capacity and overstaffing became apparent. Adjusting staffing levels to new circumstances is not only difficult due to the lack of a social 'safety net', but it would also impair the company's ability to cover the full scope of business. As process chains are interrupted, interfaces need to be re-defined and employees retrained and encouraged to become more autonomous.

The endeavour to adapt an East European company to the new conditions is complicated by the functions that companies used to perform beyond their actual business, which in market-orientated countries are the responsibility of the state, local communities, and various other service providers. In a Russian *kombinat* in the chemical industry, for example, approximately 2200 (or fully one-third) of the 6500 employees are engaged in what may be considered unrelated social services such as kindergartens and hospitals. And, due to stretched financial resources and a lack of relevant experience among authorities and civil servants, this cannot be changed immediately. Thus, the combine was privatized with the condition that social services continue to be maintained for a three-year period.

In the light of these peculiarities (unheard of in most market economies), the co-operative relationship with the East European partner has to be formed in such a way that restructuring requirements are kept as low as possible and company performance is protected from being dragged down by these cumbersome factors.

There is a range of possible relationships between western and eastern partners. On one end of the range, a pure supplier relationship is possible for raw materials and for low-quality standard products, such as steel for some segments of the building industry. The western customer, however, has to exert influence even in a pure contractual relationship to obtain quality assurance and support for optimizing the material flow. Beyond this, the western partner is not involved in the restructuring of the East European company. It is not always clear whether the cost advantage is based on a labour cost advantage or is to be blamed on lack of cost transparency.

At the other end of the range would be a single sourcing policy under which the western partner is advised to seek control over its East European partner. The impetus to obtain a controlling interest is heightened when the value added by the East European partner is high, because this intensifies the risk that factor cost advantages will be outweighed by such drawbacks as poor quality, unreliable deliveries, or excessive total cost. This is what the western partner hopes to prevent by means of restructuring.

Normally, the cost of restructuring should be covered by short-term cash flows due to the high levels of uncertainty, but that gives rise to the critical question: what is to be the subject of the co-operation and restructuring? In restructuring a large *kombinat*, the cost could more than offset the advantages of interlocked value chains. So, instead of co-operating with the large *kombinat*, the western partner should be eager to circumvent the restructuring need by establishing a joint venture to which the *kombinat* only contributes the subsidiary or division that the western partner is interested in. This is what has been done with the Russian *kombinat* described above.

In practice, this selective approach to a joint venture has proven to be appropriate for performing the necessary restructuring activities at a cost that can be amortized over a short period of time. In the best case (which should be pursued in negotiations), a zero-based approach results in a company of optimal size. On the basis of sales forecasts, the manufacturing facilities are blueprinted. Then the 'upstream' and 'downstream' activities are followed and the overhead is identified. The western investor supplies capital and machinery. The East European partner provides the right number of employees, and, one hopes, the best qualified. Since the management of the *kombinat* will also want to claim the most qualified employees, it is often difficult to reach agreement on this issue.

Forming a new company on the premises of a *kombinat* would be a viable situation. However, this can only happen if the management of the *kombinat* supports the idea; otherwise materials and supplies would be difficult to obtain. As the support of the *kombinat*'s management is one of the key success factors in a joint venture, management's goodwill should be secured by a minority stake. In addition, it has proven workable to lower the purchase price and instead give the management a share of future profits. But, if at all possible, legally and otherwise, the western investor should secure a controlling interest in order to accelerate restructuring.

The executives of Agrana, the Austrian sugar and starch producer, speak from experience when asked about the disadvantages of a joint venture in the course of an on-going privatization. In 1991, Agrana acquired a 49 per cent stake in a joint venture that it co-founded with Hungrana, the Hungarian starch monopoly, in which Hungrana contributed its total assets. As Agrana was fully aware of the risk that Hungrana might sell its 51 per cent stake, Agrana insisted on a stipulation that all changes in company policies require a 75 per cent majority vote. Two years later, the Hungarian government sold this Hungrana holding to one of Agrana's main competitors, the Belgian company Amylum. The Belgians assumed that they would control the joint venture with their 51 per cent interest until they found out about the 75 per cent regulation. From then on, both competitors only co-operated reluctantly.

Western investors are at risk of being suddenly confronted with conflict when the partner has not yet been privatized or has been sold through a 'voucher privatization' where shareholders cannot be identified. A German industrial refrigeration company minimized such risk by securing an option on the shares of the Czech joint venture partner in the event that the latter would be put up for sale. This approach is recommended if a local partner is needed or if establishing a joint venture is the only legally possible form of collabouration.

A possible change of ownership of the joint venture partner is not the only potential source of material risk. The partner's credit standing, for example, can also be problematic. There have been instances in Eastern Europe where local companies, because of poor credit rating, have had difficulty in contributing urgently needed capital.

Because the necessary mechanisms for assessing the creditworthiness of potential partners are not yet in place, the assessment of credit rating has not yet reached the required quality in all East European countries; and a step-by-step approach to dual restructuring is recommended.

(1) The co-operation starts out as a supplier relationship, under which the emerging market partner initially produces and supplies simple parts.
(2) If the partner proves reliable, the number of relocated parts and activities is increased and the co-operation is developed into a joint venture.
(3) Meanwhile, the available western capacities for the parts and related products are being gradually phased out.

One advantage of this step-by-step approach is that the dependence on the non-western partners increases in line with their proven reliability.

In addition to the assessment of the partner's credit standing and reliability, the step-by-step approach should facilitate an early identification of restructuring requirements. Age and condition of machinery, the efficiency of processes, and the education, quality, and motivation of employees can be evaluated while performing quality assurance activities, which are also necessary in a supplier relationship.

In those cases where companies were acquired even though the western investor was fully aware of huge restructuring requirements, the ability to gain valuable market shares was the overriding factor. In 1991, for example, the German Linde AG, a producer of industrial gases, acquired a majority share in the Czech company, Technoplyn. Since then, DM 200 million have been invested in restructuring and another DM 180 million will be required. But, by acquiring Technoplyn, Linde gained 80 per cent of the Czech market for technical gases. The massive investment was considered necessary to obtain and defend this dominant market share against local competitors.

In the case of 100 per cent acquisitions, due diligence has to be performed with extreme care due to the risks involved in legal succession. In Eastern Europe, significantly more time and effort has to be scheduled for due diligence than in the West due to the inadequacy and unavailability of data. The results of due diligence determine the catalogue of representations and warranties that should be requested of the seller and that need to be agreed upon in negotiations.

The emerging market partner does not always agree to such a selective approach. The ABB example introduced earlier shows how a wide range of activities not immediately relevant for the business may be divested: prior to making an acquisition, ABB negotiated the transfer of social services with the local authorities. The commercial functions – such as the locksmith and carpentry shop and the canteen – were initially taken over but later sold.

Another approach to reducing the requirements of restructuring is the greenfield solution, although it is an approach that is rarely used in Eastern Europe. Obviously, joint ventures and acquisitions are preferred in a difficult environment, because then the western investors can rely on an existing infrastructure. In addition, the necessary approvals for land acquisition and for building are often difficult and time-consuming to obtain. As privatization progresses, the number of attractive candidates for acquisition is declining. Therefore, a growing number of 'greenfield' investments can be expected in the future.

If the optimal sizing and structure of the East European joint venture or subsidiary are evaluated and determined prior to the co-operation, organizational problems are often avoided or at least minimized, such as those that extend from excessive personnel costs associated with the social services. By the time the co-operation agreement is entered, the East European company should not number more than a few hundred employees because, once the deal is struck, the restructuring reality begins.

First, optimize functions and processes . . .

Whereas western companies have to a great extent optimized their internal functions and are now in the process of concentrating on customer-orientated organizational processes, the companies in Eastern Europe (and in other emerging markets) have to start by optimizing individual functions. The key functions are as follows.

- *Control* The implementation of cost accounting and control systems according to western standards is one of the highest priorities. New accounting methods and systems provide the cost data that are necessary to make sound financial decisions and plans. Implementation of these systems is time-consuming and requires a different mode of thinking. Cost allocation methods in Eastern Europe, for example, are currently quite rough – the total overhead of a Czech manufacturer of diesel engines is allocated on the basis of manufacturing time to just two cost centres: casting and mechanical production and assembly. A system of financial controls that also provides management with timely information is a key ingredient of success for engagements in emerging markets.
- *Quality management* The fact that products made in emerging markets hardly ever meet the quality standards in place in western markets cannot be attributed to a lack of quality control. On the contrary, major quality efforts are undertaken, but they aim at the separation of scrap as opposed to detection of causes and prevention of errors and other problems. One of the primary reasons for quality deficiencies and high scrap rates is related to performance defects in machines and equipment. Also, operating procedures are sometimes lacking. When a machine is malfunctioning, it may not be shut off, even though it produces a high proportion of defective products. This state of affairs has to be changed through an improvement of spare parts supply and through provision of quality management expertise. This does not mean 'total quality management', but initially (and mainly in production areas) there needs to be improved quality awareness among employees. They must be motivated to produce quality and not just focus on the targeted volume. Quality inspectors have to

be trained to find the reasons for failures so future failures can be prevented. In the meantime, quality issues make the on-site presence of western experts indispensable.

- *Manufacturing organization* Traditionally, East European companies have been directed towards mass-production. But, under new arrangements with the West, manufacturing has to be adjusted to smaller lot sizes and in some cases even single piece production. In order to enhance flexibility, the workshop principle – a technical concept geared to full machine utilization – has to be replaced by the flow principle, aimed at customer satisfaction and reduction of lead times. The resulting optimization of material flow does not only reduce work in process, inventories and lead times, but it also reduces the management time necessary to monitor and control the operation.

  The improvement of material flow often requires the consolidation of manufacturing areas; but, as different manufacturing steps are often performed in different buildings which can be situated some distance apart, the material flow is interrupted. In the division of a Czech metal working company responsible for materials processing, for example, 170 employees work in an area of about 147,000 square metres. In addition, pre-production and production are located in different buildings, and cut-to-size sheets are exposed to air while being transported between buildings. This means that the sheets have to be surface-treated before welding – one step which could be avoided if both steps were performed in one place. Sometimes production activities are scattered over multiple locations which can require complex internal logistics and increased management time. Ideally, a consolidation of manufacturing locations will already have been completed before the joint venture is set up so that there is only one production site to be taken over.

- *Employee motivation* Flexible production methods depend upon flexibility in the skills and capabilities of employees. Although it is necessary to reduce fragmentation of functions, the big payoff results from building efficient operations in such value-adding activities as design and production. Here, training is a very critical factor – since not all employees who have worked for the particular division or subsidiary prior to the co-operation are generally taken over by the joint venture. Those who are taken over have to perform new jobs for which they may not be suited.

- *Liquidity and foreign currency management* Working capital requirements and foreign currency issues have to be taken into account in structuring the deal. The western cash infusion is probably the only source of foreign currency in the initial phase. This foreign currency cushion has to cover the cost of imported components and all pre-product expenses until the East European joint enterprise has achieved the necessary quality standards and produces goods that are marketable in the West. In order to keep this pre-marketing phase as short as possible, quality programmes have to be put on a fast track. Liquidity management in local currency requires the expertise of western employees. Liquidity is a difficult and sensitive matter in most companies – many suppliers require advance payment and many customers do not pay on time. Due to this phenomenon and the mutual interdependence of the parties involved, bankruptcy laws are not fully elaborated and they are not strictly applied or enforced. If a company were to go bankrupt in the wake of writing down its accounts receivables, its creditors and the companies 'upstream' in the supply chain would also be threatened, and the health of many enterprises could be jeopardized. The most obvious approach to generate liquidity is to reduce the excessive inventories of semi-finished and finished products, providing that they can be sold. But issues associated with inventory can be complicated too. On the one hand, high levels of inventory are attributed to a hoarding mentality caused by perennial supply problems. On the other hand, inventory accumulates in the in-stock production due to a lack of orders. And, even if the investor did not pay for the inventories, potential disposal cost have to be taken into account.

- *Optimization of vertical integration* The high degree of vertical integration is the result of past problems in sourcing and supply. As it commonly stands now, companies not only produce their own spare parts, they also have their own fleet of vehicles for transportation and distribution. Due to the lack of logistical service providers, producing companies have to manage the whole range of logistical functions. The extent to which vertical integration can be reduced is dependent on external supply opportunities; and, if there are no external opportunities, as is the case in Russia, the only possible alternative is to spin such support activities off. This, however, impacts the company's cost position very little: when the company performing the spin off is the only customer of the unit, specific overhead cost is not reduced. The only way out is to attract additional external customers, which requires western expertise.
- *Inventory and supply management* Due to the monopolistic structure of the procurement market, an evaluation of supply and suppliers may be superfluous – there may be no other alternative than sourcing in the West, which of course places a serious strain on the company's liquidity. There are even difficulties in the supply of products which are assumed to be abundant in the target country. Although Russia has huge raw material resources, they are hardly available in the country due either to logistical and organizational problems or to the fact that they are sold in the international markets for foreign currency. Ironically, even in Russia, the only way to get the required raw materials or pre-products is often to purchase them from the West.

East European joint ventures tend to operate mainly in the national market. Consequently, they are not a big generator of foreign currency. So, the increased requirement for foreign currency and the higher cost resulting from purchases in the West have to be taken into account in the initial feasibility study.

. . . then integrate restructuring into business as usual

One of the key success factors for dual restructuring is the on-site presence of western employees during the restructuring phase – preferably in line functions, possibly as consultants. A minimum of two to three western employees is required for a medium-sized East European target company with a few hundred employees.

It is important, however, that the expatriates develop an understanding of and appreciation for the local people and act accordingly, so that they will not be rejected by locals as technocratic 'know-it-alls'. Often managers of East European origin who have been educated in the West are the best people for this kind of assignment.

The expatriates have to have high levels of authority because they are in a better position to make key day-to-day operating decisions than their associates in the West. In turn they should have a performance-related remuneration package. In order to be most effective, the expatriate managers should not operate autocratically but instead should involve local managers in the decision-making process so that the locals can eventually be placed to assume control and to make decisions on their own.

As to timing, there are certain major advantages to implementing the restructuring on a tight time schedule. East Europeans still have to develop a new attitude toward time. It has been shown that fast knowledge transfer is the highest priority for successful restructuring. So, the transfer of production, sales, and commercial expertise should be handled expeditiously by the western managers. In addition to being trained on the job by expatriates, East European managers should take part in management courses and on-site education and training at western company locations.

The adjustment of both company cultures is necessary for the progress of restructuring activities. The senior management and the work force of both companies have to understand each other's mindsets and put up new rules: Both sides have to evaluate their strengths and weaknesses critically in planning and implementing the restructuring activities. They also need to realize and understand each other's situation. Only in this way can Western and Eastern European advantages be successfully combined.

Generally, the western partner is the driving force during the overall restructuring process. The 'cultural ice' has to be broken and, once this happens, joint visions can be developed and values and standards are blended. There are, however, no turn-key concepts for successful interlocking of value chains. East European readiness has to meet with western willingness to learn and adjust. A two-day 'culture workshop' with a straightforward agenda for middle and top management and members of the restructuring project team has proven to be successful in:

- developing common understanding of the rules;
- establishing the links between dual restructuring and the overall strategy of the game;
- developing operating principles for the joint venture;
- setting strategic targets and designing plans for meeting them; and
- building personal relationships and intercultural bridges.

Value chain networking requires the installation of new interfaces and/or the reorganization of those that already exist. If the value-adding activities had previously been performed in-house, a new interface might develop at the western company's boundary adding a geographical component. If, by contrast, the value-adding activity had already been outsourced prior to the co-operation, an existing supplier relationship will be discontinued as the company embarks on a single sourcing scheme with the emerging market partner. Wherever the western company has a controlling interest in an emerging market partner who performs an activity that had been outsourced prior to the co-operation, the activity is effectively re-integrated.

The western partner wants to ensure that its existing customers are not negatively affected by the new distribution of value adding activities. Thus, product quality and delivery cannot under any circumstances be allowed to deteriorate, and consequently the reliability of the East European partner is increased if the restructuring is done effectively. However, even well-designed restructuring activities will not be effective overnight. Therefore, a step-by-step approach is advisable, and single sourcing should only be commenced after a test period. Capacities in the West should only be eliminated when the activity of the emerging market partner meets the quality standards expected by western customers.

As people in Eastern Europe have a different attitude toward time, it is important that East European employees develop a stronger sense of the importance of speed of delivery. This is the first step in reorganizing the order fulfilment process in a way that is transparent to the western customers. In the transition phase, weaknesses in the emerging market partner might have to be covered with increased lead times and/or the use of buffer stock.

If the relocated products or components are not standard products sold at fixed list prices, the order generating process will have to be improved. The poor quality of orders fulfilled by East European companies is often attributed to the fact that requests are not read carefully and thus customer requirements are not understood. The customer who consequently receives an incomplete order is annoyed over the lack of customer orientation by the supplier. Thus, at least in the initial phases, the primary customer of the East European company should be an entity inside the western company responsible for filtering orders.

Since maintaining such filtering functions is costly, the quality process in Eastern Europe must soon reach western levels. With an increasing East European share in the value-adding process, there will be a proportionate increase in responsibilities borne by the East European partner in interfacing with customers. So, again, maintaining product quality is paramount, as the relocating company seeks to protect its image with its western customers and build its image with progressively more demanding East European customers. Gradually, global responsibility for the process will be assumed by the East European company for specific products and processes. This is already general practice at ABB Zamech in Poland, for example, which has worldwide service responsibility for 200 megawatt generators.

It is possible that relocation of value-added activities may lead to idle capacities in the West, at least in the short to medium term. Examples of companies with relocation experience, however, reveal that value chain interlocking does not eliminate jobs in the West. By being able to create new mixes for East–West work distribution, the cost position of the western company improves and so does overall competitiveness. Companies such as ABB have opted for a strategic approach to dual restructuring, distributing value adding activities among companies in Eastern and Western Europe.

One big advantage of using a careful strategic approach to implementation of effective East–West reallocation of value adding activities is a smooth transition, and often additional business is generated as a consequence of improved competitiveness in the markets of Eastern Europe. In addition, resources freed through value chain networking may be creatively redeployed to help the company to expand into new business areas and markets.

When a German company in the agricultural machinery sector started producing a new generation of equipment in the German location, it relocated manufacturing of the old generation to Russia. In order to secure a spot in the CIS market, a distribution joint venture was formed with the trade organization for agricultural machinery which was in the process of being disbanded. In the production joint venture with a Russian manufacturer, the German company maintained a 51 per cent ownership position. The Russian partner contributed the production facility and the required workforce, while the German company relocated the machine tools and in addition invested capital. This was followed by a step-by-step relocation of the production process. In time, all components for the selected products will be manufactured at the Russian location and final assembly will also take place there. A two-year transition period enables the German partner to build new demand to fill his capacities in Germany. To play up the success of this endeavour and to pump up employees' involvement and commitment, the management communicated the cost advantages obtained through this new East–West work distribution relationship to the workforce in both countries and illustrated how this helped save jobs and improved the company's overall competitive position.

Dual restructuring should rank high on the agenda of top management in producing companies within the highly developed western markets. Yet it should not be the only point on the agenda – dual restructuring is not a panacea. Rather, global competitiveness in the future will require a well-balanced combination of customer focus, innovation, and interlocking value chains.

5 Dual Restructuring in Practice: Strengthen the Triad Through Growth in Emerging Markets

Richard Hesch and Stefan Krenz

The Eastern European involvement of Asea Brown Boveri AG (ABB), Jagenberg AG, and a USA-based manufacturer of electrical parts illustrates the dimensions of the decision made by many companies to co-operate with emerging markets companies. The approach used here and the results of the process show the potential opportunities and organizational issues associated with Dual Restructuring.

THE ABB CASE

Percy Barnevik, ABB's chief executive, wrote in a company report in 1993. 'In addition, products of West and East European manufacturing are increasingly integrated for export projects and thus competitiveness of a concern is significantly improved. We do not regard the opening of Central and Eastern Europe as a threat but as a historically unique chance for Europe as a whole.'

The ABB case shows how a company can continuously improve its competitiveness by integrating the value added capabilities of the engagement partners in the two regions – West and East. ABB has succeeded in developing and utilizing such staging areas in Eastern Europe since shortly after the fall of the Wall.

Unlike other companies, ABB had for a long time developed business relations in Central and Eastern Europe (Figure 5.1), and this created a strong favourable starting point for ABB's new Eastern approach. Since 1892, when ABB first co-operated with a company in St Petersburg, there has been continuous growth as the co-operation has developed. Following elimination of the barriers of communism, ABB immediately decided to build on this existing base by expanding the engagement and pursuing new opportunities. ABB's current intentions are to integrate Central and East European resources in its global network, principally by relocating production of components and systems to East European companies in which ABB holds a majority share.

The overall ABB strategy was supported principally by:

- *Development of new markets* New market opportunities have been created through production of components in the East and by the founding of country-based holding companies which coordinate the sales activities.
- *Cost-effective production possibilities* Labour intensive production of components can be accomplished at low cost due to the favourable location.

In implementing this strategy, ABB followed a standard approach, as follows.

(1) The ABB decision-makers were responsible for defining those parts of the overall process which would be produced in the East. (Interestingly, only those components which are of strategic relevance to ABB were selected – even some of ABB's core operations have been listed for relocation to the East.)

(2) In Central and Eastern Europe, partner companies with corresponding product knowledge and expertise were identified, and ABB acquired shares in them. Frequently, only certain divisions of the target companies were acquired; and, activities which did not belong to the core business (such as social services) were later privatized or sold. In locations where there

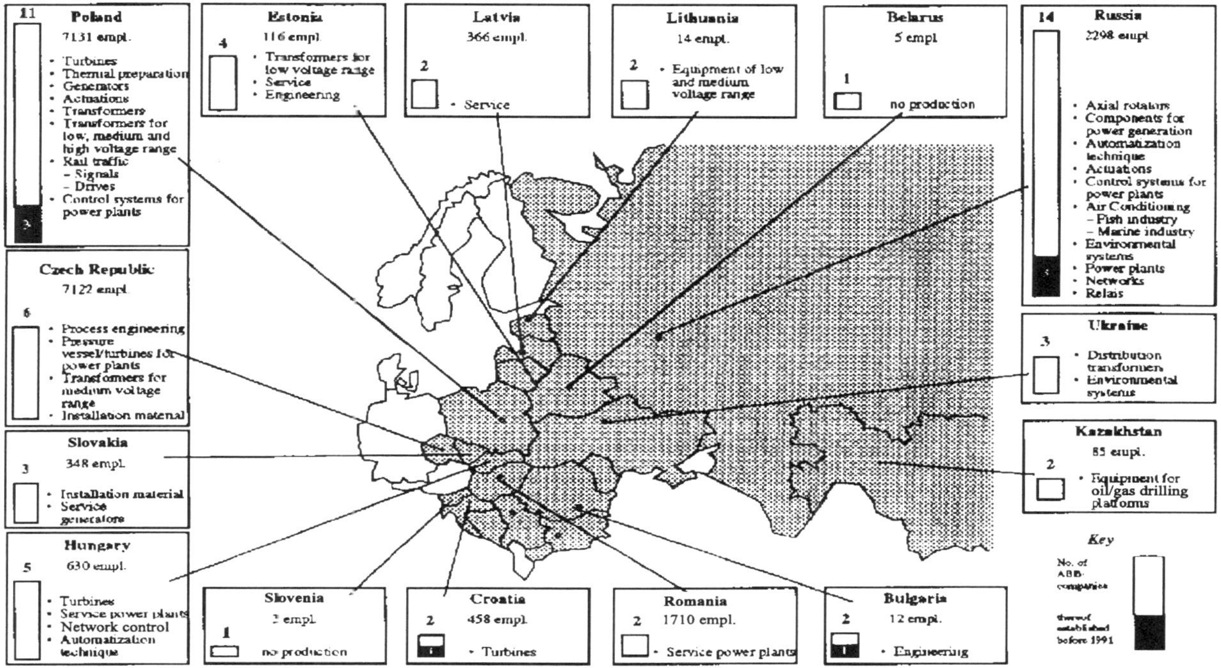

Figure 5.1 Activities in Eastern Europe

were no suitable candidates for co-operation, ABB founded new companies. This acquisition/formation phase often took only three to six months.

(3) After ABB had gained control of the Eastern management, the acquired companies were restructured quickly and efficiently under the supervision of Western ABB employees. But responsibility for the restructuring was vested in the local management. One of the main objectives in this restructuring was to eliminate deficit operations, particularly in the following areas:

- *Management expertise* Major training initiatives were launched, concentrating on finance, management, and marketing, to instil new administrative expertise throughout the organization, from the shop floor to top management.
- *Organization* A divisional organization was implemented and responsibility was consequently passed down to lower levels of the hierarchy. In some cases lean processes and material flows were introduced. The main objective was to achieve Western quality standards in these areas.
- *Reporting system* Western-style data processing systems were implemented, particular in the accounting areas, to begin to build meaningful accounting controls and timely management information.

Existing problems were not handled sequentially but were solved in parallel. As problems were addressed and corrected, however, there was a comprehensive effort in the organizing and restructuring work to develop 'model' ABB companies. Up to fifteen Western experts were in place at any one time to support the local employees, but all of the work helped to build a common knowledge base; so that, as similar problems were encountered in other ABB companies, only a short time was required for restructuring. On average, it took ABB only two years to restructure its Eastern companies.

Today, only shortly after ABB's aggressive partnership-plans were initiated, complete components are now produced in the East European ABB companies, and the production processes combine several value-added steps. A description of one operation in the wide range of the ABB/East European operations helps to explain this dramatic success over a relatively short period of time.

ABB Zamech in Elblag (Poland) was acquired in May 1990. Supplier subcontracts had been in use since 1973. But with the acquisition initiative, the ownership structure is now as follows: ABB holds 76 per cent of the outstanding shares, 19 per cent are held by the state, and the final 5 per cent are held by the work-force. ABB invested US$50 million and spent a great deal of time in restructuring an organization of approximately 3300 employees, headed by a Polish management. The company now produces complete turbines and generates annual revenues of US$120 million. The company also has responsibility for the worldwide service of 200 megawatt generators and is active in developing new technology as well as in its planning and implementation.

'Dual Restructuring' at ABB is regarded as 'job sharing,' and both partners – in the East and the West – benefit from this collaboration. If Component A (for example, a compressed air reservoir requiring high-cost welding) can be produced at lower cost in the East due to the favourable conditions in that location, the overall system increases in competitiveness – clearly, the Western company producing Component B of the system benefits from this.

It is important to recognize that dual restructuring, and the relocation and reorganization that are implied, can generally not be a static process: new products, new technologies, new market opportunities are being developed continuously. So, the value-added production and distribution chain can and should be viewed as a dynamic situation.

The strong entrepreneurial commitment and the large investment have already paid off: Two per cent (or US$465 million) of ABB's total sales in 1993 can be attributed to the production based in Central and Eastern Europe achieved with 7 per cent (14 766) of the employees. Although productivity in these areas amounted to only one-quarter of the ABB average in 1993, productivity has grown sevenfold in the meantime, and it is constantly improving. In 1993, order volume reached almost US$1 billion. It is ABB's intention to increase these figures even more. By 1997, it is projected that 40 000 employees should reach an order volume of US$3 billion.

THE JAGENBERG MASCHINENBAU GMBH & CO. KG CASE

The case of Jagenberg Maschinenbau GmbH & Co. KG shows how a company in the highly competitive machine manufacturing industry can continuously improve its competitiveness by taking advantage of a location in Eastern Europe and by developing unprofitable areas into profitable ones. This venture was an essential part of the vision of its senior management officer – Dr. Wolf-Peter Müller has noted, 'One precondition for me as the CEO was the development of an Eastern production location on the basis of the reconstruction of the mechanical engineering area in order to re-gain profitability.'

In addition to machine manufacturing, the Jagenberg concern operates in such business areas as the paper industry, foil technology, and packaging, and in 1993 it generated turnover of DM 777 million. On 1 April 1993, machine manufacturing was separated from the paper divisions and was transformed into the legally independent Jagenberg Maschinenbau GmbH & Co. KG as a manufacturing company working for the Jagenberg concern and external customers.

In the abbreviated year of 1993, the Maschinenbau GmbH & Co. KG generated a loss of tens of millions. In 1994, revenue of DM 74 million was achieved and the workforce was reduced by 20 per cent to 426 employees at year end. Eighty per cent of the revenues are generated in the production of parts and components for Jagenberg's paper production, 5 per cent in Jagenberg's other business areas, and 15 per cent in work for customers other than Jagenberg.

As has been stated, one of the key objectives in forming a legally independent unit location was to realize cost reduction and so increase competitiveness in the production of machine parts. A big problem to be faced, however, was that, in the area of conventional small parts production, small-sized manufacturers in Germany could provide the parts as subcontractors at hourly rates between DM 45 and 60, whereas Jagenberg's hourly machine rate exceeded DM 100 (without a profit margin).

It was expected that, through staff reductions and new employment agreements, savings could be realized, but improvements in these areas were not sufficient to be competitive in small parts production. This helps to explain the loss in the partial year in 1993.

Two strategic options resulted from the obvious need for action (driven from a comparison of market prices for parts production):

(1) to close down the conventional small parts production at Jagenberg and outsource to a small-sized independent company. Under this scenario, the paper production units could purchase the parts directly from the *Lohnfertiger* and not pay the comparatively high margins that would be involved with Jagenberg Maschinenbau. This, however, would result in an overall decline in sales for the company as a whole;

(2) to try to undercut the prices of the German supplier. It was this consideration that initiated the whole concept of expanding to the East, because there were no other savings to be realized from the old location and satisfactory opportunities were not to be found in such locations as Portugal, Great Britain, or Italy. This approach followed the basic principles of dual restructuring:

- Functions to be relocated were identified immediately – those parts of production that could be handled with relatively easy-to-operate conventional machinery but had high-cost personnel requirements. As indicated, price competition is high in this area, yet expertise demands are relatively low. This made the functions especially amenable to relocation.

- Immediately after the separation of Jagenberg Maschinenbau GmbH & Co. KG, a search began for new locations in the East for parts manufacturing and assembly, and the area targeted was the Czech Republic. In 1989, Jagenberg had already outsourced the maintenance of packaging machinery to affiliates of the Czech-based Milcom concern. Thus, some kind of co-operation and a basic mutual understanding was already established. A strong track record in machine manufacturing and an acceptable geographical distance guaranteed that the labour cost advantages in the East European country would not be given back in the form of excessive transportation and handling cost.
- At Jagenberg, dual restructuring became a top management issue: in May 1993, senior executives of Jagenberg Maschinenbau visited the Czech Republic and Slovakia to analyse four candidate companies.

The selection criteria for determining adequate companies were defined in detail, and the partner company finally selected had to be prepared to satisfy the criteria and to reconfigure its workforce into a newly established joint venture company. In addition, Jagenberg required a partner that did not operate in high-volume serial production but who instead excelled at producing in small lot sizes, from 1 to 20 units. (These small lot sizes are generally required from Jagenberg as a producer of special machinery.)

In addition, Jagenberg wanted to bring in its own machinery from the West as a fixed asset investment into the joint venture. With the unrelated relocation of two other companies in the Jagenberg group, Jagenberg's machine tool capacity was vastly underutilized and was available for transfer to the East. So there was a proviso that the Eastern partner would need to have sufficient space available to accommodate the new equipment of the joint venture.

Another important selection factor was that the partner company should be located in an industrial area so that it could provide access to a workforce sufficient for later expansion plans. In addition, productivity in the form of working speed, reliability, and quality were analysed in detail by the top managers during their site visits.

After four companies had been visited – two companies in the Czech Republic and two in Slovakia – the responsible Jagenberg managers decided on Vuma in Nové Mesto, Slovakia. Vuma's special strengths are prototype construction and small lot sizes, and already the employee base had been reduced by 75 per cent – from 2000 employees initially to 700 employees in 1993 and then to approximately 500 employees in 1994.

The geographic distance was also acceptable – a distance of 1400 km to the parent company in Neuss with good roads ending within 15 km of Vuma's company gates. (Another firm that had been visited was situated in the Tatra mountains and had poor traffic conditions, especially in the winter.) One final favourable consideration for the Vuma site was that a nearby machine tool company was scheduled to close and would therefore provide a large number of skilled workers.

After these managerial site visits, Jagenberg's board of directors approved the joint venture in June 1993, and Vuma Jagenberg – the name of the joint venture – received the first test orders soon thereafter. Although regulations have since changed, it was the case at that time that foreign companies could not establish a company in Slovakia without the participation of local partners. So, it was agreed that Jagenberg would initially hold 20 per cent and Vuma would hold 80 per cent of the shares in the joint venture. It was further agreed, however, that Jagenberg Maschinenbau GmbH would acquire 51 per cent of the shares as soon as productivity reached the target ratio of 1 to 2. (It was 1 to 4 at the time the joint venture was formed.) The reason for this approach was Jagenberg's principle of caution: Jagenberg transferred the necessary machinery to Vuma, but made it available to the joint venture on a lease basis. When it holds the majority share, Jagenberg Maschinenbau will enter the equipment on the books.

There are huge cost advantages: Jagenberg pays a transfer price of DM 23 for each production hour (compared to DM 60 in the West). On top of that, an amount equivalent to DM 2 is paid for transportation.

Twenty-five Vuma employees were brought into Jagenberg. The head of production was one of the employees, and that guaranteed that only the most qualified were selected. Currently, the total joint venture work force amounts to 73, but a workforce of 120 is planned for the near future.

Restructuring has been carried out by Jagenberg Maschinenbau quickly and efficiently. A West German expert was assigned to the joint venture company for six months in order to supervise the installation of equipment, to instruct the employees and acquaint them with Jagenberg's policies, and to organize production. The same accounting system as in Jagenberg Maschinenbau was replicated in the joint venture, and a premium wage system was introduced in order to improve motivation and productivity. A simple, but efficient management information system was developed, and plans call for major system enhancement once Jagenberg obtains the majority share. Vuma Jagenberg was also linked to the German data processing system for order management.

Materials management has been the only major problem. The Slovakians had difficulty purchasing raw materials, so Jagenberg Maschinenbau had to organize a weekly truck transport of finished parts from the Slovakia site to the parent company. On the return trip, the truck is used to distribute the semi-finished parts.

There were two primary reasons for the fast increase in new employment: First, a large volume of finished parts for paper technology could be produced at Vuma Jagenberg; and, second, Vuma Jagenberg was a prime location for the assembly of components for the packaging industry.

Jagenberg Maschinenbau exemplifies successful cost-induced dual restructuring. Market considerations were of minor significance in the decision to relocate, even if it turns out to be the case that the market develops appreciably. Now that the venture is in place, it appears that Vuma Jagenberg might profitably be used as a staging area for additional relocations in the East.

Today, the test production of major parts in the East is showing a 60 per cent cost reduction compared to current costs in the West.

According to Jagenberg Maschinenbau, the key success factors were:

- initially relocating only uncritical, labour intensive parts of the operation, and that only after previously testing for quality;
- integrating local employees adequately and using their contacts to the maximum;
- separating from the parent company only those areas that needed to be separated.

Today, Jagenberg Maschinenbau is in the enviable position of being able to offer its customers finished parts and components with a competitive blending of Western and Eastern cost positions. Compared to 1993, current losses have been reduced by 50 per cent and a balanced result is the objective for 1995. This would be considered excellent compared to the losses experienced by the industry as a whole in recent years. While it was painful to make the personnel reductions that helped bring operating losses under control, the cuts were considered necessary by the parent company. Even representatives of the workforce are convinced that less, but competitive, work is better than continuous losses and eventual bankruptcy. It turns out that this careful approach positioned Jagenberg well for future adaptation and growth.

Dr Wolf-Peter Müller, when asked what he would have done differently, replied, 'Perhaps our approach was too cautious and we should have tried to acquire the majority right from the beginning. In addition, as to space, we are already at the limit of our capacity – a larger building would have been more suitable. Otherwise we would approach things in the same way.'

THE ROTATION INC. CASE

Rotation Inc., a US manufacturer of various types of electrical components and motors, was in a critical condition. Revenues had been stagnant at US$1 billion for three years, and the COGS (cost of goods sold) versus sales ratio had risen from 70 per cent to 80 per cent, indicating a considerable erosion of margins.

Top management decided to cut costs significantly by divesting non-core business areas and by optimizing the manufacturing effectiveness for the core businesses, rather than use traditional cost cutting techniques. As Rotation was already manufacturing some of its components and motors in Mexico, they investigated the possibility of increasing manufacturing in Mexico to determine if this would increase manufacturing optimization.

A.T. Kearney supported this study, and the results led to a typical dual restructuring.

Project execution

Investigators collected most of the data through personal plant visits. Data was gathered from smaller plants by having managers complete a questionnaire. Investigators also interviewed these managers by telephone to avoid misinterpretation of the questions and to capture information 'between the lines'. Spread sheets were then used to facilitate the computation of different models.

Key data were:

- output levels
- capacities and utilization rates
- up-time
- cost structures
- material flows in the production network:

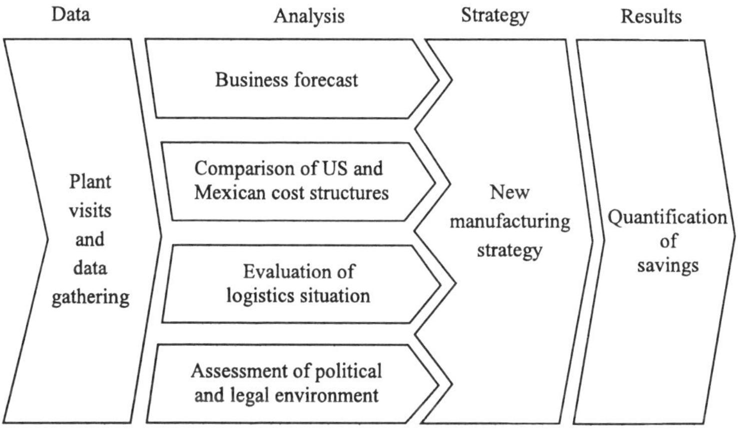

Figure 5.2 Project structure

The main decision variables for a new manufacturing strategy were found to be:

- a forecast of business development
- a comparison of US and Mexican cost structures
- an evaluation of the logistics situation
- an assessment of the political and legal environment (Figure 5.2).

The business development forecast was readily available and indicated slightly increasing sales for most items for the next five years, supplying a good estimate of the required production capacities. Another important item was the plants' cost structure (Figure 5.3). The two main results were:

- apart from materials, which are difficult to influence except possibly by using a supply management approach, labour is the largest cost category;
- labour cost is significantly lower in Mexico than in the United States both as a percentage of the cost structure and in absolute terms. (Labour costs per hour varied

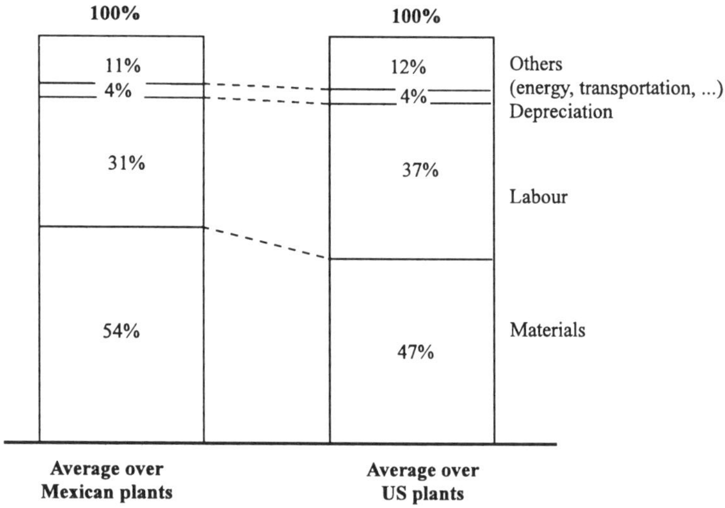

Figure 5.3 Cost structure

between US$12 and US$36 in the United States and between US$2 and US$7 in Mexico.)

Analysing the logistics situation, in particular the internal materials' flows, was essential for quantifying the additional logistics costs resulting from a shift of production to Mexico.

Analysis of the political and legal environment produced important information needed for strategy development:

- Research on the risk of unionization and on the ability to manage large plants showed that 400 to 600 hourly employees is the ideal plant size in the USA;
- For some products and processes larger plants in Mexico were feasible without any loss of efficiency.
- The Mexican border is currently preferred over the interior for new plant locations, but the interior would probably be favoured for future development.
- Since Rotation already had some experience in Mexico, using these existing locations for moves into Mexico was a critical advantage.

Following this approach, labour intensive manufacturing processes for basic products were assigned top priority for a shift to Mexico (Figure 5.4).

For the production of electric motors, the processes assigned to Mexico were:

- rotor assembly
- starter assembly
- motor assembly
- motor testing.

The low labour-intensity processes with high moving costs:

- bracket and die-casting
- stamping

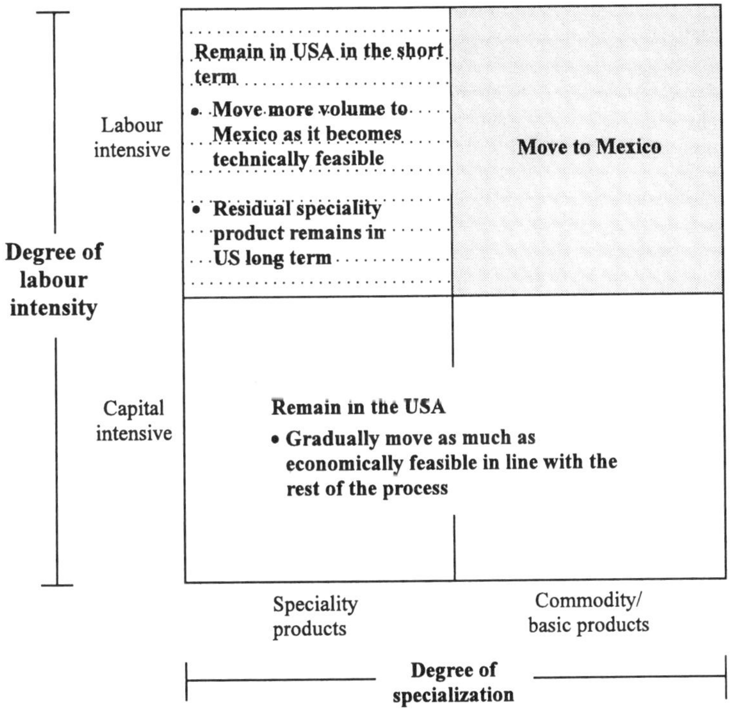

Figure 5.4 Basic strategy portfolio

- annealing
- terminal box fabrication
- stamped frame/shell fabrication
- slitting,

were recommended to be kept in the United States.

To accommodate the relocation of manufacturing processes, it was necessary to close US plants and open additional Mexican facilities.

Using the computer model to determine the differences in cost and productivity and taking into account increased transportation costs due to changes in the flow of goods, Rotation was able to quantify the savings created by the new manufacturing strategy.

The shifting of production to Mexico was expected to take place over five years. Figure 5.5 shows how costs were anticipated to decrease in line with progressive shifts of production to Mexico.

A cash flow analysis for the entire company, taking into account once-off changeover costs, demonstrated that the

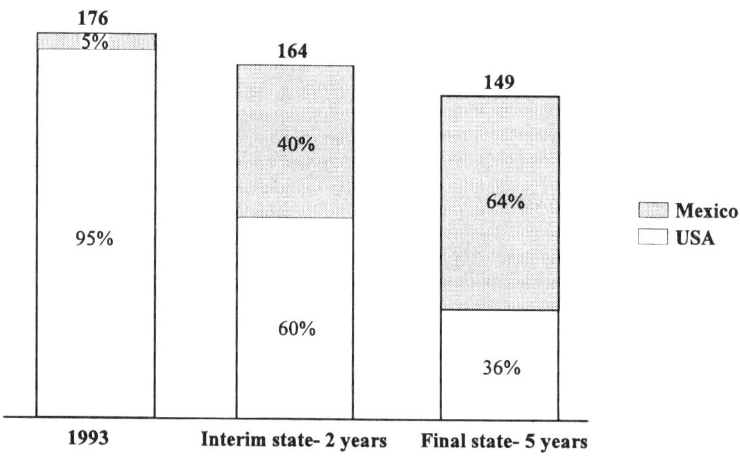

Figure 5.5 Costs of goods sold (US$ million) – example: motors

strategy would start generating a positive cash flow after one year. Furthermore, the ratio of cost of goods produced to sales was expected to drop to 75 per cent after three years and 70 per cent after four years, bringing it back to the level of the late 1980s.

6 The Outlook: Transfer of Industries and Regionalization of the World Economy

Fritz Kröger

Through dual restructuring, Eastern Europe, Latin America and South-east Asia will be the major recipients of foreign direct investment in coming years. This renaissance is fated to be, despite the fact that public opinion has devalued these regions and their capabilities. Hyperinflation, massive pollution, old bureaucracies, and high crime rates are the modern plagues that afflict these regions, especially Russia.

If one compares the Triad countries and their neighbouring regions on the basis of quantitative data and judges their attractiveness according to the 'sources of strategic competitive advantage' applied by Lester Thurow, Eastern Europe, for example, takes a strong position in comparison to other world regions. It has the natural resources, the human capital and the knowledge background as well as the technological and industrial infrastructure.

- In natural resources Eastern Europe offers prime energies like gas, coal, uranium and crude oil – 30–40 per cent of the world's natural resources. In iron and non-iron metals it has 20–25 per cent.
- With regard to human capital, the position of Eastern Europe is even stronger. The Communist regimes of Eastern Europe were known for making extraordinary investments in education, especially in natural sciences and technical and engineering studies (Figure 6.1).

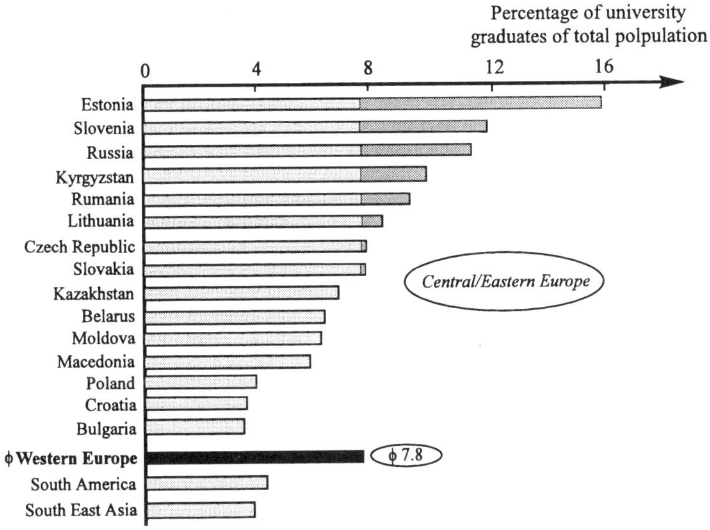

Source: Emerging Market Economics Report 1993, The World Competiveness Report 1993

Figure 6.1 The high percentage of university graduates in Eastern Europe

Everyday contacts with business leaders from Eastern Europe confirm the human resources aspect. In addition to their strength in natural sciences, which has been documented by worldclass performance in aircraft, aerospace industries and medicine, Russian executives impress us by their broad and deep education in the humanities. This educational background in combination with the enormous labour cost advantage opens up a tremendous potential for productivity improvements.

This productivity potential was demonstrated during the restructuring of former *kombinats* in Russia, Hungary and Poland. Per unit cost reductions of 40–50 per cent were achieved even though absolute labour cost increased by 20–40 percent from 1993 on.

The comparison of the industry portfolio for Western Europe with Central and Eastern Europe shows a similar overall industrial structure – coinciding with a comparably

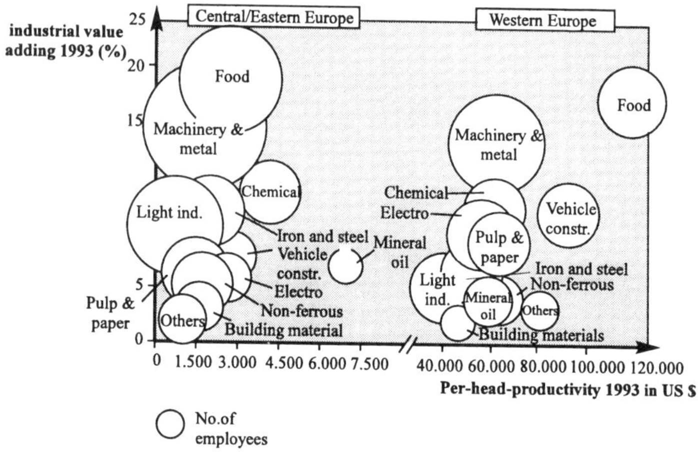

Figure 6.2 The similarity of industry portfolios in Western, Central and Eastern Europe

developed infrastructure (Figure 6.2). It is precisely these structures which open enormous potential for dual restructuring in nearly every industry. Potential investors find industry traditions and structures that have been cultivated over more than 50 years, although the level of development might differ from industry to industry: wood and furniture, textiles, paper, large parts of the iron and non-iron metal-processing industry, shipyards, major parts of the steel industry and the machinery industry are candidates for dual restructuring (Figure 6.3).

A frontrunner in this trend is the reorientation of global sourcing activities, especially in the European machinery and automotive industries into Central and Eastern Europe.

Dual restructuring in general is a chance for all Triad regions to participate continuously in the global creation of wealth even though their cost position and lack of flexibility may not allow for competitiveness in the near future. Dual restructuring also presents a unique opportunity for developing countries favourably situated near those Triad giants. Their need for fresh capital and jobs is as obvious

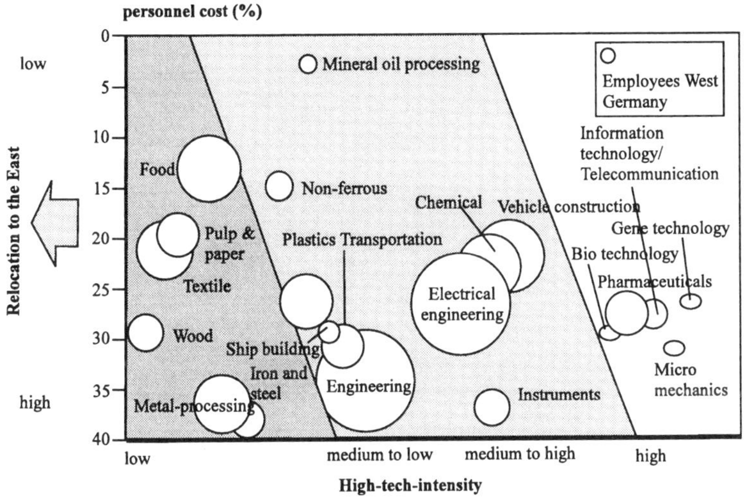

Figure 6.3 The trend to relocate to the East

as their ability to provide cheap labour now and to become attractive markets later.

Although in human resources and industrial infrastructure one emerging region might rate higher than another, cultural similarities, geographic proximity and therefore logistics complexity add convincing arguments to the choice of the respective 'dual restructuring region'.

What does dual restructuring mean to the Triad regions? Triad markets will naturally expand into their neighbourhoods, driving regionalization of the world economy.

- Japan will no longer be the only industrial nation in Asia Pacific. With the 'little tigers' in two different stages of development, some – such as China – providing cheap labour, and others already developed, this whole region is bound to boom.
- Europe from the Atlantic to beyond the Urals will gain strength from dual restructuring. During the later phases these countries will grow closer together than ever before

in history. If leaders of all involved countries and companies take the chance to stake out an economically strong and larger Europe, they will be able to take care of whatever problems may linger in the CIS states beyond Russia.

These states are now in a critical political situation mainly triggered by economic troubles. They are logically tomorrow's partners for dual restructuring once Eastern Europe has caught up with the West.

- We find a similar situation in the USA – NAFTA seems to be a huge step forward towards integrating the southern part of the western hemisphere into the enormous American and Canadian markets – but it is only the first step. Once Mexico, through NAFTA and all the advantages that accrue to it, has established itself as a less shaky economy than it has been recently it will be a reliable bridgehead for future positive developments in South America. The MERCOSUR and other states will become natural partners for dual restructuring of US as well as Mexican companies.

So in this context it seems Goethe was right when he reminded people of the wisdom of not looking for solutions beyond one's own horizons but to concentrate on the familiar: 'Why roam so far afield . . . ?'

Will all this happen without hardship for all parties involved? Certainly not. These Triad economies will require extreme flexibility and will experience great discontinuities. There will be major layoffs of people in low value-added, labour-cost-intensive functions in traditional industries. On the other hand there will be enormous expansion in the higher value-added functions like marketing, sales, product development, and logistics coordination. Those more complex parts of the dual restructured value-added chain will have to serve the greatly increased markets of the new regions – for example, 780 million in Europe as a whole versus 350 million in Western Europe. To make this possible, governments will have to invest heavily in the education of younger citizens and in the permanent upgrading of all workforces. On the other hand there will be a trend toward de-industrialization of former industrial regions to a higher level of service industries, a trend already quite advanced in North America.

The greater the significance and impact industrialization has had in the respective Triad country, the more activity and innovation are required to accept and to reorientate to the new basis of employment.

To co-ordinate and conduct those adaptation processes, close communication and co-operation between government and industry are required. We recommend industrial policy models such as MITI in Japan as possible role models in this context.

A stable affluence in the primary regions and a growing wealth in the emerging regions are definite prerequisites for political stability. So dual restructuring might be a concept for long-term wealth equilibrium although it requires tremendous flexibility and effort on all sides.

Dual restructuring is the imperative for the future. Companies that recognize and utilize this trend quickly and before their competitors will have decisive competitive advantage for a longer period of time.